photos
for the future

SUTTON PUBLISHING

THE HISTORY CHANNEL.

First published in the United Kingdom in 1999 by
Sutton Publishing Limited · Phoenix Mill
Thrupp · Stroud · Gloucestershire · GL5 2BU

British Library Cataloguing in Publication Data
A catalogue record for this book is available from the British Library.

ISBN 0-7509-2435-7

Title page photograph: This is a photograph taken about fifty years ago at Newcastle Town Moor 'Hoppings' – an annual event begun as a temperance festival in 1882 and which has continued every year since (apart from war years). About one million people attend the ten-day gathering which can truly be called a cherished part of the history of the area, hence the submission of this item for the 'Local History Project of 1999'. (J. Trevor Williams)

 ALAN SUTTON™ and SUTTON™ are the trade marks of Sutton Publishing Limited

Typeset in 11/14pt Gill Sans.
Typesetting and origination by
Sutton Publishing Limited.
Printed in Great Britain by
The Cromwell Press, Trowbridge, Wiltshire.

Contents

Introduction

One might well ask why the photographs in this book are called *Photos for the Future*. We have called this collection *Photos for the Future* because they began not as an idea for a book but as The History Channel's project for the Millennium – a competition which aimed to assemble the photographs of our viewers as a record of the twentieth century for future generations.

What is unique about this collection is its origin. These photographs haven't come from professional photographers or the picture archives of newspapers and magazines. These photographs have come almost entirely from the personal family photo albums of people all over Great Britain.

Clearly some of these images were in fact taken by a 'professional' – the local photographer who offered households that couldn't afford the luxury of a camera the novelty of a family portrait, a photo of a father or son called to arms, or a record of that family outing to Bournemouth in a charabanc.

But whether these images were professionally taken or just a family snap, what makes them interesting is their place not only in the personal history of these individuals but also their place in the shared, often commonplace experiences of everyday life for ordinary people in the twentieth century. In assembling this archive we were constantly struck by the recurrent themes – the small family business, the first holiday abroad or the first family car – that have formed part of our collective experiences as participants in our century's history.

The captions that accompany these photographs were written by the people who sent us their photos. These captions contain some wonderful stories and were equally important for us because the judging for the competition was based not only on the quality of the photograph but also on its historical significance. Many of these texts reflect the fact that history isn't just about the kings, queens, prime ministers and generals we study in school, but that we too as ordinary individuals have been history makers at the heart of the twentieth century.

We hope that *Photos for the Future* will become an historical reference for future generations. Above all we are glad that the project has encouraged people to go back to their own personal family history. We hope that in so doing they have discovered a bit more about themselves and that they will pass it on to their daughters and sons, who will in turn do the same for their children.

Geoff Metzger
The History Channel

Acknowledgements

The History Channel would like to thank the following organisations who cooperated with us on the project to make it such a success: Beamish – The North of England Open Air Museum, Birmingham Central Library, Bournehall Museum & Library, Cadw – Plas Mawr, Dover Museum, Flagship Portsmouth, Letchworth Museum & Art Gallery, The Museum of Liverpool Life, The People's Palace, The Potteries Museum & Art Gallery, The Royal Armouries, Leeds, West Berkshire Museum, Oxo Tower Wharf, London, and all the local libraries up and down the country – for providing exhibition venues and communicating the project.

We would also like to thank:

The *Express* for getting behind the project and helping to publicise it;

The Campaign for Museums – 24 Hour Museum and the Victoria & Albert Museum for holding virtual exhibitions on their websites;

The Historical Association, LEAs, and all the County Councils especially Suffolk for helping to communicate the project;

Alf Wilkinson and Graham Goodlad for their advice in involving schools;

Our panel of judges – Professor Bill Speck from the Historical Association, Peter Clifford from Sutton Publishing, Mick Lidbury from The *Express*, Jax Connelly and Paul Prowse from Hulton Getty Picture Collection, Geoff Metzger from The History Channel.

And finally we would like to thank all the companies and individuals who worked so hard to make the project happen – Nicki Harris, Anna Brady, Michelle Reed, Jo Mitchell, Centurion Press, Imagecare, Euroworld Direct Marketing and the project's researchers – Rebecca Blech, Anna Morozgalska, Mark Loader, Lucy Harris, Steve Livesey and Katerina Pishiris.

family

My father Albert and Uncle Dave (fourth and fifth from left respectively), flanked by their close chums and associates (my honorary uncles!) proudly bestride their Swallow Gadabout motor scooters in Brook Road, Bootle, in 1950. For me this shot symbolises the British postwar spirit of 'have-a-go' camaraderie and enterprise which ushered in the era of the self-made man challenging our class-ridden business establishment. How ironic to note, as we approach 'total European union', that our economy was soon to be eclipsed by our former adversaries – rather as these bikes were by the Italian Lambrettas and Vespas. (Allen 'Gaz' Gaskell, **Winner**)

I like this photograph because it is a picture of my grandfather at the age of 13 in 1939, when the British ruled India and the Second World War began. He had led a privileged life from birth, and regularly went hunting. Three boars have been killed, servants carry spears and the young boy on the left of the picture is my grandfather. The plump man with a turban next to him is his father. A friend who had an interest in wild animals is the reason they went hunting that day. He killed the first boar. Another boar came to avenge the slain, which my great-grandfather killed. The third boar was found. My grandfather had sharp eyes, a steady hand and could shoot more accurately than any man. (Puja Babbar, Queen Elizabeth Girls' School, **Secondary School Winner**)

This picture of my great-grandparents surrounded by their family was taken at their sixty-fifth wedding anniversary in 1968. It's a beautiful example of a marriage that lasted so long – something which is rare today and will surprise many in the new millennium. It shows how much my great-grandparents valued the family, which is furthermore shown by the fact that they had fourteen children! Although large families weren't uncommon then, they are definitely rare today, the average family consisting of only two children. This is a shame as large, united families are a wonderful example of strong, moral values. (Bérengère Lepine, St Paul's RC School, **Secondary School Winner**)

The 10-year-old Czech refugee in the picture is my Gran starting a new life in England. One of ten thousand Jewish children saved from Nazi death camps by British rescuers, she owes her life to a man called Nicholas Winton. Of forty-five relatives, thirty-six were murdered including her parents so she stayed in England, grew up, got married, had two children and four grandchildren. I am alive because people cared for a young refugee. We must try to stop wars and ethnic cleansing from happening and always be there for refugees. They must have hope. (Amy Marie Rowlands, The Grange School, **Secondary School Winner**)

This is of personal value to my family because it is a photograph of my grandmother, Edna Ruby Harbach, taken when she was 16 years old. It is of historical value because it was taken in 1932 at a time when women were beginning to get more job opportunities. It also shows examples of 1930s hairstyles, clothing and machinery. It would be useful to people in the future because people might want to research 1930s clothes or hairstyles and also people would be able to see how teapot spouts were made and the type of machinery used. (Amy Blackwell, The Grange School, **Secondary School Winner**)

This shows my second cousin and his family on the Ocean Liner Express leaving Waterloo for Southampton on the way to New York and a new life in California, 1952. After my cousin's demob from the Navy, they found themselves, like many young London families after the war, with few future prospects and so accepted the offer of a house and employment in Los Angeles. Most people are aware of the immigration into Britain but this photo is interesting as it illustrates that life was not easy here in those years and many Britons emigrated to other countries. (Sophie F.K. Robertson, Ursuline High School, **Secondary School Winner**)

This photo of my great-grandfather, with my grandfather and his two brothers outside their cottage in Abercregan, South Wales, was taken in 1926 during the Great Depression. He was a School Manager, Hospital Governor and County Councillor. He organised soup kitchens to feed the children of the local villages. The entire village relied on the mining industry, and children (including those in the photograph) started down the mines at 14 years old. When the mines closed, the entire population dispersed, these cottages were demolished and the slag heaps grassed over. An entire way of life has vanished. (Daniel Wilcock, St Paul's RC School, **Secondary School Winner**)

This photograph shows my parents getting married in 1979. It has personal value to me as it was the first mixed race marriage in both of their families. I think it is of historical relevance as mixed race marriages were still uncommon then. I think this is useful to future generations because it shows how racist people have been in the twentieth century. (Asha Styttard, Coopers' Company & Coborn School, **Secondary School Winner**)

This is my grandad, Dennis Hart, sitting outside his lodgings in Cwmaman, South Wales. He was 19 years old. He was called up at the age of 18 in May 1944. He wanted to join the Navy, but had to become a 'Bevin Boy' miner instead. Grandad was there for three years and lodged with a local widow whose husband had known Keir Hardie. He was a journeyman down the pit, where conditions were hard. At this time, he was an amateur bantamweight boxer and once fought at Caernarvon Castle. After this he worked at GAC, Brockworth. (Sam Piper, Brockworth School, **Secondary School Winner**)

The picture shows my grandfather, aged 7, with his mother, father and grandfather, 1912. We can see how fashions have changed, and that family photographs were rare and more formal than they are nowadays. Two years after this photo was taken, the First World War started; as it ended – four years later – my great-grandfather died, and at the age of 13 my grandfather had to work through his school holidays to help pay for his education. This is of interest to future generations because a posed photo like this does not show how hard life was in those days. (Olivia Goodman, Ashford School, **Secondary School Winner**)

Above: This is a photograph of me and my older brother (holding Teddy) at Stonehenge. It was taken and developed by my father in 1954. I was 3. The monument was completely unfenced then and although it is summertime (I am wearing last year's Startrite shoes with the toes cut out) there is no one else about except my mother in the distance. I can remember the magic of being among the huge stones. I love the composition of the picture but it makes me nostalgic for the time before crowds and mass travel. (Ms Guinevere Vaughan, **Runner Up**)

Right: At our family home this photograph was taken of myself and my sister Lorraine who was born without arms and legs, eleven months prior to myself in 1961. Our mother took thalidomide to help with morning sickness during her pregnancy. The thalidomide disaster went down in medical history as a huge mistake; it seems the drug was never tested properly. Hopefully physicians and pharmacists have learnt from the error and will never prescribe the drug to pregnant women again. In the picture, Lorraine is wearing standard issue wooden legs. She ended up in a wheelchair. (Karen Braysher, **Winner**)

This is a photo of my Uncle Harry. It was taken in the '30s and shows him sitting astride a Douglas motorbike and sidecar in Cheltenham promenade. Such new means of transport gave young men the opportunity to travel further to gain employment and meet new people. In the case of Harry, it was to meet his future wife in Birmingham. The railings in the foreground were removed during the Second World War for the war effort. (Mr M.W. Meredith, **Runner Up**)

This is a photo of my grandfather (left) William Henry Lovering, with his son Teddy and two friends in Bow, East London, in about 1912. He was born in 1877 and died in 1948 in Pitsea, Essex, where he had bought a smallholding. They borrowed the goat and made the cart for Teddy who died aged 7 from flu. He had nine children with my grandmother, seven of whom lived to adulthood. Gran lived to the age of 92 and died in 1970. (Patricia Skeels, **Runner Up**)

My father had a holiday in the mid-1920s on the Isle of Man and this snap was among his keepsakes. I do not know who took it. The steamers are belching particularly black smoke and I am told there are horse-drawn trams there now, instead of the rank of landaus. Steamers still run from Douglas to Fleetwood, but I do not think that they would be allowed to produce such black smoke. (Mrs E. Watson, **Runner Up**)

This is a photograph of my great-grandparents. They are going out for a day to the coast on a charabanc. The two children in the centre front are also family members. Their names were Arthur Hill and Harriet Hill and her maiden name was Honeyball. The coach was hired from Cunnmore Motor coach company and the photograph was taken in England. (Yvonne O'Donoghue)

This picture of my mother, Lilian Frances Soames, was taken in London on 24 June 1916. She was 19 years old on the occasion of her participation in one of the first Alexandra Rose Days. Ladies who volunteered designed and made their own dresses using the wild rose theme – my grandmother considered the dress too short and insisted my mother attach a false hem. The hat, stand-up collar and tray were all decorated with roses. The sash ribbons were scarlet and white. (Mrs Iris Charos, **Runner Up**)

Orlando Rowley was killed in August 1904 at the Sneyd Colliery near Burslem, Stoke on Trent. While working in the Cockshead seam with two brothers named James and Daniel Gidman, there was an explosion of gas. All three were badly burned and they subsequently died from their injuries. The photo places a face to the all too often forgotten tragedies that befell miners and their families and in itself is a poignant piece of Stoke on Trent's social history. (Geoffrey Mayer, **Runner Up**)

Her Majesty's Welsh Guards, passing the Victoria Memorial for their first guard mount at Buckingham Palace. My father is second from the left, behind the officer. My father Robert Henry Long (born 23 April 1901) had a very hard life under my grandfather who ran a pub and two removal companies in the East End of London. Of Irish descent, 6 ft tall at the age of 13, he became thoroughly fed up grooming horses at 4.30 a.m. under the totally unnecessary demands of his father. Borrowing his elder brother Edward James's birth certificate, he ran away with friends to join the Irish Guards. The Irish were not recruiting and the recruiting Sergeant Major persuaded them, emphasising all the anticipated glamour, to join the Welsh Guards. (Denis G. Long, **Runner Up**)

This is a photograph of my mother taken in 1926 at the age of 16. She will be 90 next April. She wanted to be a film star. Her mother opposed her ambition. She married a print operator, has five children, nine grandchildren and six great-grandchildren. She still does the cooking and no-one is allowed in the kitchen at Christmas. I hope she feels her family have given her happiness over the years, and are a satisfying replacement for her youthful film ambitions. (Dame Shirley Oxenbury, **Winner**)

My family, in 1957. At the time, my father was stationed at RAF Seletar Camp in Singapore. The baby in my mother's arms is my brother and the occasion is the day of his christening. We are a Catholic family and lived through an era when large families for some were the norm. A time too when mixed marriages were viewed with scepticism. The millennium holds significant meaning for my widowed mother as she was married on New Year's Day 1943. (Yvonne Marshall, **Runner Up**)

This is a picture of our daughters Katy (then aged 4) and Joanna (then aged 3). Their excitement was caused by the McDonald's hamburgers and the McDonald's paper hats they had just been given. BUT THIS WAS MORE THAN TWENTY-SIX YEARS AGO! Long before McDonald's ever set foot in this country. Our friend, Herb Lotman, owner of Keystone Foods Inc. in the USA is the largest supplier of hamburgers to McDonald's. On his visit here in 1973, he brought us a box of 144 hamburgers, together with hats and other McDonald's items. So they had the country's very first McDonald's! My wife was also given a silver Ronald McDonald's watch, usually reserved for McDonald's millionaire franchisees. (Robert Vince, **Winner**)

This is a photograph of sisters Annie and Nellie, and the year is 1913. Nellie, on the left, was my great-aunt and Annie was my grandmother. Nellie never married and when their brother John Edward McDonald took office as Mayor of Dewsbury in the early 1950s, Nellie served as his Mayoress. The family were Irish immigrants who had settled in Batley during the 1880s, and they and the large Irish community in which they lived were extremely proud when 'one of their own' was privileged to serve in this way. (Mrs Sheelagh Davidson, **Runner Up**)

My mother, Mabel Radford (now deceased). Having studied various paintings and books about the turn of the century showing aspects of family life, I decided to take some pictures to record a glimpse of that epoch of the twentieth century. This picture shows one of their past customs – clay pipe smoking (even the ladies smoked them). This photograph, taken by available light and sepia toned, gives one an idea of the life (and perhaps difficult times) of the working class in the earlier part of the twentieth century. Maybe this is a photo to look back on in the future. (Bill Radford, **The *Express* Winner**)

Here are John and Jessie Finnie, my grandparents, in Watson Crescent, Edinburgh, before 1914. This photograph was kept in a family album and always known as 'a guid hing oot the windae'. In the days before radio and television, people would get their own 'soap opera' by watching their neighbours and chatting to passers-by. The picture was taken by an itinerant street photographer who would have developed it there for a small fee. Notice also the coloured varnished paper on the windows, which gave colour and privacy. Nowadays, the street is lined with cars and there is little scope for activity. (Sandy Currie, **Winner**)

This is my maternal grandmother, Mrs Beatrice Blanche Sanders, taken in Monghyr, India, in 1910 with her first-born child, Arthur Stafford Charles, and an Ayah. My grandfather, William Arthur Sanders, was sent to India in 1908 as a factory engineer by W.D. & H.O. Wills, Imperial Tobacco. He sent for his 18-year-old fiancée who had never travelled beyond Bristol before, and they were married in the English chapel in Calcutta, straight from the ship. This photo is sad for two reasons – because all boys had to be sent home to England to be educated and because at 6 months old, Arthur – along with all the other babies in the jungle station – died of dysentery. The small cemetery is still in Monghyr, full of tiny graves. A tragedy of the Raj and a vivid reminder of its dangers for white people. (Mrs Jenny Farmer, **Runner Up**)

Shortly before the outbreak of the Second World War, my great-grandmother Emma Williams celebrated her 94th birthday on 4 May 1939 by taking her first flight, and I was privileged to fly with her, together with my parents. It was a birthday treat arranged by the local press as she was the oldest inhabitant in our steel town. Her only disappointment was that the pilot refused to loop the loop! She was an ex-publican who survived four husbands and the Blitz, in that order. She died peacefully in 1943 aged 98 years. (Arthur Colburn, **Winner**)

This photograph was taken in 1908 a few months after my mother, who is the baby in the bassinet, was born, together with her parents, her grandparents and her great-grandparents and various other members of the family. The pram in which my mother is sleeping is now to be found in St Fagan, the National Museum of Wales in Cardiff. The bridge that can be seen in the background is the viaduct that carries the Snowdon Mountain Railway on its journey to the summit of Snowdon, the highest mountain in Wales. (Gordon Parry, **Runner Up**)

My parents at a holiday camp in the 1950s. A redcoat is presenting them with a modern vacuum cleaner as the prize for the 'Ideal Husband' contest. In these days of package holidays to the Mediterranean and other even more exotic destinations, people often sneer at holiday camps, but in their time they provided great family holidays, when such breaks were considered a luxury. (Janet Dodson, **Runner Up**)

This is a picture of my Uncle Tom taken in 1981. He was a wonderful raconteur with a great sense of humour and a deep roaring laugh. He lived all his life on a small farm in Northern Ireland. As a young man, he worked as a forester and later took over the running of the farm. His way of life has ended with his generation. (Jon Martin, **Runner Up**)

This photo was taken on 22 July 1911 at the Coronation of George V and Mary. My mother (aged 11) is the fourth child from the left on the fourth row with a male teacher standing immediately behind her. My father is on the third row from the top, slightly to the right of the lady teacher wearing a very fancy hat and slightly below two boys in Panama boaters. He is wearing a dark cap with flowers tucked in the brim of the cap on the right-hand side. I don't know whether they knew each other at that time as they attended different schools, and I am sure they would never have realised that fourteen years and a world war later they would marry. (Margaret E. Roberts, **Runner Up**)

The most striking aspect of this 1950s photo is the sheer abundance of smiles, despite their obvious poverty. My father is the small boy (aged 10) at the front, with his four (later five) sisters and mother. This hopfield in Guildhurst, Kent, was one of their many seasonal employment areas. All family members would help. Age was no barrier – as long as hands could pick. The working-class life which is depicted here reflects the incredible strength and unity of the family. This holds significance for me as it is a far cry from the materialistic lifestyles we lead today. (Mandy Baker, **Winner**)

This picture shows my great-grandparents with their car in 1927. I think that the car is the most important invention of the twentieth century. It has revolutionised society, giving people the mobility to work, shop, go on holiday and live where they choose. Over this century, the motor industry has provided millions of jobs, especially in industrialised countries where it is a major part of their economy. However, the massive growth of cars, from 600,000 in 1911 to 500,000,000 today has brought the negative consequences of pollution, change of land use, traffic congestion and fatalities on the roads. (David Dawson, Fulford School, **Secondary School Winner**)

Samuel Cox, my gunsmith grandfather, with his wife, two daughters and four sons. From left to right the sons are Charles, Frederick, Arthur and Richard, all of whom followed my grandfather into his business. The little girls are Jessie and Nellie, my mother. This group was taken in Grandfather's garden in 1890 when Mother was 3. (Colin Reid, **Runner Up**)

This is a photograph of my great-grandpa, Gilbert McKeller. He was born in 1882 and died in 1927 at the age of 45. He lived in Northbank Cottage, Portencross, before the murder took place. Later on, he moved to Egypt and became Chief Officer in the Egyptian Government in 1912. Gilbert married Elizabeth Cornelius in 1916, and had a daughter named Elizabeth after her mother, but is known as Betty. (Julie Lorraine, West Kilbride Primary School)

My grandmother, Alice Gronow, was an exceptional human being whose gift to the world was that of humility and affection. She was always from my childhood my inspiration at times when, in foster care as a child, all I had was her image on a sepia photograph to remind me that I did have a family. She set up a field hospital in Caerffili to care for the victims of Spanish flu, that dreadful illness that robbed so many in the valleys of loved ones. She in turn was to follow shortly after, another victim of the flu she had nursed so many through. (Andrew Carreg, **Runner Up**)

This is a picture of my great-great-grandma. She was 'Miss Mary' – one of the Eight London Belles. In the early twentieth century she travelled and performed virtually all over the world, including Russia and America. They later became known as the Bluebell Girls. (Lauren Blunden, Lammas School)

This is my great-auntie Sheila (aged 17); she was Miss Manchester. It was 1945 and the war had just ended. Her grandmother with whom she lived (as her mum died prior to the war from TB and her father died at sea during the war) was very angry that she had the nerve to enter a beauty pageant. Sheila was then working for Kendal Milne as an apprentice; she was invited to take part by the actress Margaret Lockwood who came into the store just to choose someone to enter. That is how she became the photographer's model. She now lives in America. (Claire Boyes, Brownhill Primary School)

The young woman in the photograph is very attractive, showing vitality and a love of life. She was my mother. She died in 1934 aged 25 from tuberculosis. The illness was bred in conditions of poverty but it spread through all levels of society. Tuberculosis remained a killer of both old and young until, under the National Health Service, treatment became free to all. The number of sufferers declined until it was thought the illness had been eradicated. However in the past few years it has, sadly, appeared again. (Peter Tickner, Brockworth School)

This is a picture of my father, mother and mum's brother, Les. It was taken in Broadstairs before my parents married in 1937. As mum and dad had wanted to go on holiday together and as they weren't married at the time, my Uncle Les had to chaperone them to ensure they didn't get up to any 'hanky-panky'! (Valerie Scouler)

My father in 1919 in Totterdown Street, Tooting, outside his parent's flat. He was 8 years old. Dad used to tell me that on Sundays (and maybe Christmas) it was customary to wear 'Sunday Best'. I do not know if this was his best suit, maybe not as his sleeves appear to be a bit too short. (Valerie Scouler)

Because of the two world wars the twentieth century has been noted for being the very worst for war, carnage and human despair and misery. This photo of my ten-day-old granddaughter cradled in her father's arms gives a message of hope, renewal, love and care. Taken in October 1995 after forty years of peace in Britain, the hope is that it will remain so for the twenty-first century. For me, the greatest miracle of all is that I was privileged to be present at her entry to this world. I hope the world will be kind to her. (Mrs Dianne Martin)

My Uncle Eric (right) and two friends in 1944. They were all determined to be pilots and opted to join different services to fly. They enjoyed the inter-service rivalry and aircrew camaraderie that existed at the time combined with the adventure of learning to fly as young men. It shows us today a friendship that stretched across different services in a time when everyone was united in a common cause. (Jacque Dowdall)

The person on the left of this picture is my father. In 1928, he was a patient in Wolsingham Sanatorium, Co. Durham, suffering from tuberculosis. It seems that the beds are outside the ward, as fresh air and rest were the order of the day. When my husband contracted TB in 1953 he had bed rest for six months but by then streptomycin was administered so his TB was cured. In recent years we have heard of minor outbreaks but screening helps to prevent its spread. During the twenty-first century let us hope that diseases now incurable will be conquered. (Mrs E. Watson)

My great-grandmother stands on the left of this picture at the back with her domestic helper Susan. As a farmer's wife she was kept very busy with domestic chores. These would include making butter, cheese and ale. Great-grandmother made all her own clothes and clothes for her children as did most people of that time. She must have spent a lot of time and effort working on them. They look very intricate. I choose this picture because its clarity shows this intricacy in their clothing. I think future generations will be fascinated by this. (Pete Curtis)

My maternal grandparents, both deaf since babies, my grandfather from meningitis, my grandmother from an accident. He was taught privately, she went to a state school for the deaf in Brighton. Her speech was better, taught by feeling balloon vibrations when words were spoken against it. In her 80s, now a widow for many years, a test showed that she had partial hearing and she was given aids. Hearing was like a strange language, one she was now too old to learn, but she recognised laughter. So many years wasted. I wonder how my mother learnt to speak in such a silent household. (Mrs Wendy Batchlor)

A photo taken in 1962 of my parents with their first car – a Morris 10. They are pictured in High Wycombe, where they had driven from Portsmouth to visit my mother's brother, who was stationed at the Royal Air Force base there. It was the first major journey undertaken in their new car, and a great event for them. In the 1990s, when we have two- or three-car families, and everyone takes the car for granted, motoring has lost the sense of occasion that it had in the 1960s. (Julie O'Neil)

This is a photograph, taken in front of Mother's home in Dover, of my parents' wedding in August 1913. My father was on HMS *Indomitable*. His best man, a shipmate, subsequently married his sister, one of the bridesmaids. Three of the men not in uniform worked on the cross-Channel boats. Mother's bearded father was quartermaster on the SS *Engadine*, on which he served in the Battle of Jutland, when converted to a seaplane carrier. By 1919 mother's brother John had been killed on the Somme, two bridesmaids had married, one to a Frenchman and one to a Canadian. (A. John Andrews)

My grandma Freeman (nearest the rear) with a friend and one of her five daughters in the driving seat! The chauffeur is not in the picture. (George Brian Kelsall)

My mother at Christmas 1907 when she was almost four months old. Her name was Connie Packwood. She was born in September 1907 and died in September 1993. (Mrs L. Hogan)

This is a photo of my grandfather taken by my father before the Second World War. I found the negative among my father's belongings after his death and used it to make a print. This may not be historically significant, but it makes me smile. I hope others find it amusing. (David Lay)

This is my grandad, about to ride the replica of a ship called the *Mayflower*. The original carried Puritans who moved from England to America in 1620 because they weren't allowed to practise their religion in England. My grandad was on the ship because he was a doctor and a sailor. The people on the ship lived like the pilgrims had over 350 years ago. This may be of interest to people in the future because the Pilgrim Fathers created the US constitution. Also, his clothes are what the pilgrims would have worn. (Phoebe Platman, Lauriston School)

My father John Thompson when he was stationed in Mhow, India. He left Mhow on 27 March 1930 to go to Bombay, which he left on 21 October by boat. It travelled approximately 300 miles a day entering the Red Sea on 26 October, passing the African coast on the 28th, Port Suez on the 31st, Port Said on 1 November. He passed Algiers on the 6th, Gibraltar on the 7th and reached Southampton on 11 November 1930. He was a member of the 1st battalion, the Bedfordshire and Hertfordshire Regiment, Aldershot. (Mrs L. Hogan)

These slums were demolished in the 1930s. Our house had no bathroom, and water was boiled in the scullery copper. The toilet was in the garden. The people in the street were poor, and unemployment was rife: the local pawnshop was always busy. We went to the bakers and greengrocers on Saturday nights for stale bread and cakes, and specked fruit. We had to wait until all customers were served and the shutters half down. (Thomas Sayers)

This is a picture of my grandfather William Charles Swann. It was taken in the late 1920s in the village of Middleham. This was the last horse and trap to be used in the Northallerton postal area, and probably the last one to be used in Yorkshire for the delivery of mail to the dalesfolk of Wensleydale and Coverdale. (William J. Parker)

My grandma was about 5 years old when this picture was taken. She is not in the picture as the people in the middle, the man and the woman, are her grandparents and all the thirteen people are their children. My gran, now 73, told me that they lived in a two-bedroom house and they all slept top to tail, and her gran used to hand bake two loaves of bread a day. Today we think life is hard, but at least we have a Tesco nearby. Sadly there are only three still alive but I bet they had some fun times and some great stories to tell. (Charlie Leighton)

'Having a wonderful time if only the wind would stop blowing!' This is a photo of my wife, Betty, writing postcards watched by our son, Michael, at Southport in 1963. The sun shone quite a lot but the wind was strong and chilly so we always had to find a windbreak of some kind, hence the bushes. (Ronald Pears)

This is a photograph of my great-grandad. His name is Harold Mayer. This was taken during the First World War. His number was 21178 – a private in the Bedfordshire Regiment. I wonder how he must have felt leaving his wife and family to serve at the front. Luckily he survived the war and rejoined his old trade as a miner, still facing danger in his everyday life. (Gregory Mayer)

This is John Stokes who was born into a family of travelling showmen in South Wales. He left home when he was 16 to go into the travelling show business for himself. Some of his many enterprises were a snake show, a roundabout turned by a small pony from the middle, Town Crier, a coconut shy and various other stalls. He broke horses and was a horse dealer, a scrap metal merchant and also ran a travelling boxing booth. He did some boxing himself and would take anyone on, offering them a golden guinea if they could knock him down over three rounds. When he got too old to box, two of his sons took over. It is said he never lost his golden guinea. The jackdaw he is holding in the photo was tamed from the wild and never left him until it died. (Ben Stokes)

A very good friend and neighbour died on 30 January 1999 aged 82. He and his family had lived opposite for forty years. John Edward Colyer was born in 1917. He enlisted on 28 August 1935 at Dover and served in the Queen's Own Royal West Kent Regiment where he achieved the rank of Corporal. He often spoke of his wartime experiences when asked and had earned many medals – the Africa Star, Defence Medal and General Service Medal. He was also in Malta during the siege but somehow missed out on the medal. The photo was taken just before the war. (Mr F. Gregory)

The O'Neil family at Queen Elizabeth's Silver Jubilee, 1977. There was a fancy dress parade at our local street party in Highgrove Road, Portsmouth. I won a moneybox for my Queen of Hearts costume. It was the first time I had won anything, and I was quite gratified! There was a real sense of community during the festivities, which you don't often come across these days. (Julie O'Neil)

My daughter Lexi was born on 26 March 1993 with Down's Syndrome. Even ten years ago her future would have been bleak. Here you can see her enjoying the results of integration as she goes to Copnor Infants School, Portsmouth, to take part in their 'Other People, Other Places' day. (Kate Saunders)

This is our 6-year-old daughter, Amy, proudly dressed in traditional Welsh costume, to celebrate St David's Day, 1998. Amy attends a Welsh medium school and enjoys the celebrations that go along with the honour of being Welsh. (Tracey Bassett)

This is a photograph of my mother dressed as Britannia in the village of Toddington, Bedfordshire, for the procession commemorating the Jubilee of King Edward VII on 6 May 1935. (Mrs D. Rigby)

This picture was taken in 1998 at Kasmu, Estonia, and shows me, aged 50, happily reunited with three generations of my family. My mother came to the UK as a refugee in 1947 when the Baltic states were annexed by the USSR. She was single and I was adopted soon after birth. I loved my adopted parents but wanted to find my blood kin. It took me over twenty years, and I never met my mother who died before I traced her. In 1998 I found my family thanks to information gained from the Internet. (Ms Hilary Bird and Anneliese Meikar)

This photo was taken on 12 August 1956. It was the house warming of Sheila and Michael Fitzgerald at 5 Haymeads, Welwyn Garden City, also Sheila's 21st birthday and christening of their daughter Miriam aged two weeks, their fourth of five children. They remain the first occupants of this early council estate originally designed by Ebenezer Howard. (Sheila, third in from the left, Michael second in from the right at the back). Back then your first home was where you stayed to bring up a large family with the help of relatives close by. Rent was £1 19s. 'Waspy waist' belts were 'in' and smoking wasn't dangerous then. (Connie Fitzgerald, **ntl Winner**)

My maternal great-grandfather proudly poses with his Spanish wife and family, including my grandfather (on the far right) on their return to England in 1924 after a life spent in Gibraltar, except for active service during the Great War. Army married quarters were not big enough for his large family (not all pictured). They were accommodated in a draughty Nissen hut in Catterick, North Yorkshire, something that certainly wouldn't happen to a regimental Sergeant Major approaching the Millennium. (David Manners)

This photo depicts rural life in the Suffolk village of Kedington. It was taken just before the Second World War and is of my father George Orriss. It shows that even when working in the fields, a dress code applied (notice the fob watch). How blissfully unaware they were of what was about to happen in the ensuing years. (Ms Monica Davis)

This photograph of my grandparents was taken in the late 1920s by a seafront photographer in Scarborough. Some of these photographers had dressed up monkeys which would sit on your arm for the photo. The photographs were displayed outside the Sun-Ray kiosk on the promenade later that day and could be purchased if you liked them. As cameras have become commonplace, the seafront photographer has become a thing of the past. (Zoë Stead)

This was taken at Yarmouth in the summer of 1930. It shows Jean with her mother, a memento of a happy day. The family day trip to the sea was an annual event, catching a train after 11 a.m. when tickets were cheaper. In those days, people never had holiday gear but rather, I suspect, they wore their 'Sunday Best' – after all outings were a special occasions. The bathing machines behind us were used to change into bathing costumes with decorum before venturing into the sea. (Jean M. Pond)

This photo was taken in the 1920s. It shows my two female cousins Phyllis and Josephine waiting in a carriage to be taken for their ride by the Ayah (their Indian nanny). They are the daughters of Lt Nicholl. (Betty L. Freeman)

This photo of my Uncle Lt William Nicholl (left) was taken in the 1920s in India. He served with the British Army in India, and later with the Indian Army. It shows my Uncle on his day off. The other man is the local District Commissioner whom my Uncle escorted to villages within the civil districts. (Betty L. Freeman)

My father George Blackburn and his half-sister Ethel dressed for the funeral of Queen Victoria. He was apprenticed as a fitter and subsequently became an improver when his wage would be increased. His employers dismissed him and his fellow improvers instead – such was unemployment before 1914. Unable to find work, he enlisted in the Royal Engineers and spent four years digging tunnels and laying mines, at Vimy Ridge. In 1922 he met my mother in Preston. During the Second World War, they lost their home to a parachute mine in 1940 and on three subsequent occasions by incendiaries and bombs. He died in 1957. (Audrey Coles)

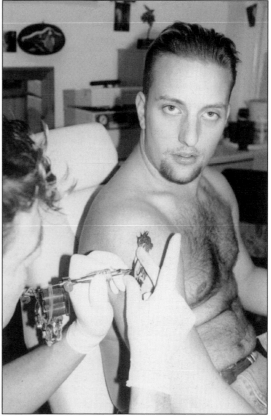

This is my husband Graham being ritualistically gowned for the Chairing Ceremony at the Painscastle Bardic Eisteddfod on 15 May 1999. Graham had already won twenty-four bardic chairs thoughout Wales, yet all these chairs were won for Welsh poetry – apart from this winning poem which was written in English. It is rare to write literature of such high calibre in both English and Welsh. Therefore it is even more unique for a poet to win chairs in both languages in Wales. (Mrs Jean Williams)

This photograph shows my youngest son Daniel having a tattoo on his arm. In Chichester The Hornet Tattoo Studio was quite a shock to the cathedral city when it first opened! Even though this art form is frowned upon by many it is still a very important part of our history and culture. In the early part of the century seamen and the military adorned themselves with tattoos – now a broad spectrum of our modern society display this permanent body art. (Richard Cooke)

This is a photo of my mother in a 'Miss Butlins' line-up when she was 15 years old, taken in 1954 on her first family holiday after the Second World War at Clacton Butlins Luxury Holiday Camp. Clacton Butlins was demolished in favour of lucrative housing developments. This unfortunate fate is the disease of the twentieth century. (Elaine Ingram)

This photo was taken in 1969, a few years before I took up photography seriously. The picture is of my family: father, mother, two sisters and little brother. It was taken in Regents Park, during a visit to London Zoo. This is the only good picture that I have of my family during these early days and it will be forever etched in my mind. (Tony Jones)

The photograph, probably taken during the First World War, shows my mother, the girl on the right, with her parents and sisters. Like thousands of other families from East London, their only holidays were hop picking in Kent. Everyone did their share of work. Their temporary home was the bell tent. Notice the pile of firewood and the makeshift frame from which cooking pots were hung over the fire. When hop picking became mechanised, an era of working-class history was lost. This is the only photograph of my mother with other members of her family. (Henrietta Howe)

My great-grandma, her sons John and James, and the twins Agnes and Helen (Welsh). It was taken in Glasgow in 1928. There are four generations in this group. I hope future generations of my family will be blessed with such memories. I am now in my 82nd year. (Mrs Agnes Power)

This is a photo of me and my mother taken in 1969 on my second birthday in our basement flat in Hove. My mother was one of the many thousands of single parents of the 1960s. When I was 4, my infant class was on the ground floor of Connaught School and my mother attended further education classes on the floor above. She gained qualifications for university entrance and I used to attend the lectures with her in my half terms, sitting quietly at her side, drawing and colouring. We both became successful professionals and are very proud of each other. (Julie Anne Bromley)

My husband's father Harry Moss in about 1900. I myself never knew him as he had died before I met my husband, although I knew my mother-in-law very well. He was a Liverpool man and he worked for the White Star Line as a purser on the big liners. He was purser on either the *Mauretania* or the *Aquitania* at the time when the *Titanic* was being built. He was asked if he wanted to go on her as the purser. As he was very happy on the ship he was on at the time, he turned the offer down. The hand of fate? Everyone knows the rest. (Mrs Ellen Moss)

This is a picture of my elder brother Peter in 1934, showing me the model London bus he made which had recently won him first prize at the Model Engineers' Exhibition in London. It was taken at our home in Ealing. The model was made from simple materials: for example, the tyres were originally the rubber rings used at that time to secure umbrellas and the seat covers were from the linings of fountain pen boxes. It illustrates the high standard that could be reached in the days when there were few, if any, model shops. (Edward Jerome Rycroft)

My grandparents on holiday. The picture was taken in the summer of 1901. It shows my grandparents Robert and Agnes Fowler with their first six children. They are on a working holiday hop picking, the only holiday that they could afford. The picture was taken at Paddock Wood in Kent. While on holiday the whole family lived in one tent. What a difference their holidays were compared to holidays nowadays. (Mrs Jean Rundle, **ntl Winner**)

This photograph of my mother's family on one of their trips to Epping Forest in around 1906 contains my mother, grandparents and great-grandmother. The only non-relative is a school friend. Gran's brother, Sam, drove the cart and as Gran and her sister married two brothers, also pictured, it was a close-knit family. They all lived in Bethnal Green where I was born and lived until marriage. I now live in Loughton which is probably where the photograph was taken as Gran used to speak of getting water at the fountain. This is still there but is not in use. (Mrs E. Haynes)

This is a photo of my great-uncle Tom, the gentleman with cap and jacket. The postmark on the original is 1908. It was my uncle's public house in Liverpool and as you can see, even in those days, they served coffee. Unfortunately I do not know the name of the pub. (Mrs Rosemary F. Abraham)

This is a photograph of my husband, Robert Brown. The year was 1955 and he was on leave from the Army. The Suez crisis was imminent and he was due to be sent out there. He was very proud of his MG Magnette – bought for £40! He is outside the Sun Inn in Ireby, Cumbria, which was, for many years, run by his family. (Mrs W. Brown)

This is a photograph of my father's christening on 27 July 1912. The one-month-old baby is hidden within the huge pram while his mother, Bertha Burgis, and his grandfather, Edwin Burgis, after whom the baby was named, look solemnly at the camera operated by his father, Cecil. I like Bertha's suit and the hat is fit for Ladies' Day at Ascot. Thirty years later, she became the only granny I have ever known and we were great friends, but fashions had changed by then. (Mary J. Morris)

This photo shows, from left to right, my grandfather, Uncle Sam, Uncle Alan, me, my mum, and Auntie Lucy. My Uncle Alan, during the First World War, was a Marconi Wireless operator, he was torpedoed three times; the last time they were rescued by a German U-boat which dropped them off at Cardiff, South Wales. (Mrs Rosemary F. Abraham)

This picture was taken in August 1938 near Arundel – halcyon days, but not for long. My father (far left) with two friends and his first car – an Austin 7. My father lived in Coventry, and said that in the town there was a car maker for practically every letter of the alphabet; this Austin 7 is typical of the years just before the Second World War. In the 1930s, smoking was far more prevalent and socially acceptable, as can be seen in the photograph. (Karen Parsons)

This is a family photograph taken shortly after the Second World War (c. 1949). Life was beginning to return to normal and my father and uncle had taken me for a day's fishing into Lincolnshire. We lived in the industrial city of Sheffield where the rivers were too heavily polluted to support fish life, especially after the war effort. In 1999, ironically, fish are beginning to return to the Sheffield rivers whilst pollution from agricultural chemicals is now a worry in Lincolnshire. (David Chaplin)

My son Ross has cerebral palsy. He was brain damaged at birth in December 1989. He is a brave, bright, courageous boy who has worked hard and overcome many obstacles. He brings sunshine to everybody's lives and is an inspiration to many disabled people throughout the world. As a reward for his courage, we took him to swim with the dolphins in 1997 which was a fantastic experience. This is truly a twentieth-century achievement, not only for Ross, but for other disabled people. A book about Ross was released in September 1999, called *Unbroken Spirit*. (Karen M. Watchus)

My grandfather Allan Marshall, suitably dressed and mounted, ready to lead the annual parade of the Ancient Order of Foresters through the village of Cambuslang, Lanarkshire, c. 1900. The Foresters – a mutual aid society – provided member families with some insurance against unemployment, sickness and old age – pre-DSS and NHS. For fifty-four years, Allan Marshall looked after the horsepower at the local Turkey Red Dyeworks – from the huge Clydesdale horses to the pony pulling the manager's surret. He and his wife celebrated their diamond wedding in 1934. He died in 1937 at the age of 90, leaving a family of ten, with eighteen grandchildren. (Allan Marshall)

These are my grandparents Ivan Patrick and Grete Clarke, born in York and Copenhagen respectively. They met and married in Paris in 1929. When the Second World War broke out, they were interned as foreign nationals in the town of Vittel. During this time they converted to Catholicism. They were repatriated in 1944. I took this picture in Leeds in 1992. My grandfather is wearing his papal medal. For me, it is a picture of the things my grandparents believed in, like marriage, religion and love. They were married for sixty-five years. Patrick died in 1994 and Grete in 1998. (Helen Clarke)

This photo represents a wonderful memory of when our beautiful dog, Bertie, won his first ever competition, to take pride of place on the front cover of a Pet Prints calendar. Seated with him is my daughter, Sarah. All my family travelled with Bertie by train to the Hilton Hotel in October 1997, where a host of judges, including DJ David Hamilton, had the difficult task of choosing just one dog out of twelve attractive beasts. It will always be recorded in our photo album for future grandchildren, especially as it was our dog who won the day! (Mrs Sally Ling)

This is a photo of my mother and me walking along Ramsgate Promenade in 1946 when I was 2. The turban worn by my mother was fashionable at the time, but it also served the useful purpose of concealing the rows of pipe cleaners with which she curled her hair. My parents would take my sister and me on the steam train from London and my mother would have a damp flannel to wipe clean the soot from our faces and hands. With the rhythm of the train we would chant 'We're off to the sea, We're off to the sea'. (Linda Bromley)

Taken in 1910, this photo shows my great-grandfather Thomas with six of his nine children outside their home in Leeds. My grandmother May (back left), now aged 102, is the only one surviving – come the millennium, she will have lived in three centuries! Women's lives have changed greatly over the century. Large families like these were common in the early part and attitudes to pregnancy were very different. The mother Sarah could not be included in this picture as she was expecting her next baby and it would have been unseemly. (Maggie Smith)

This is a photograph of the Skutt family, taken approximately 124 years ago. My wife helps an old lady who is aged 89 and it is her father who is the young lad in the back row (Albert). He died aged 87 on 11 October 1975. The picture was taken in the family garden at Polden Road, Salisbury. I re-photographed it after I saw it hanging on the wall and sent it, with her permission, as a classical Victorian photo. (Mr F. Gregory)

In this photo, taken near Porth Wen, Anglesey, in February 1997, my daughter Megan aged 10 is blowing me a kiss. My wife, Laura, is standing in an archway of a disused limekiln. This picture represents to me both an end and a new beginning. An end to an industrial era which introduced this century and a new beginning reflected in Megan's youth and spontaneity. The farm in the background represents a continuity through time which we all share. (Heinz Frommann)

This photograph shows my aunt in her nurse's uniform, during the First World War. After the war, she became chief stewardess with the Cunard Line and married an American millionaire whom she met on board. Sadly she died, probably of cancer, while still young. I remember as a young child going to a huge house in London for her funeral. (John Lloyd)

A seemingly idyllic rural scene before the First World War. My father is the youngest boy in the picture. However there was an outside toilet and water had to be drawn by hand. The five here were the youngest of ten children, not uncommon in those days, and my father's clothes were mostly hand-me-downs. My grandfather was a cabinetmaker, and my grandmother took in washing to help make ends meet. In Herefordshire there were four school terms a year, children returning to lessons in August, and breaking again in the autumn to help harvesting hops, to supplement the family's income. (Mr K. Preece)

On Wednesday 19 May 1999, my mother, Lola Ayonrinde, became the first black Mayor of Wandsworth. She is the first black conservative Mayor in the whole of England and Wales. The first female Mayor of Wandsworth was Miss Gwynneth Morgan in May 1969. Over the last twenty years, more women have become involved in politics. They have been able to establish themselves as powerful role models for young women today and have proved that they are just as capable as men at being good leaders in society. My mother is grateful for the opportunity to become Mayor because it gives her a chance to achieve all her ambitions and set an example to those who have multi-ethnic backgrounds. (Oyebolade Ayonrinde)

My grandma, in 1948. During and after the Second World War, Grandma kept an allotment with pigs, chickens and vegetables. Our job, as grandchildren, was to collect food scraps in a bucket from the neighbours for the pigs. Grandma had a licence to kill the pigs herself. This is not allowed now. She hung the carcasses from large hooks on the landing ceiling along with strings of sausages. She made local news because she'd made the longest unbroken string of sausages from the pig gut! (Janet Rees)

This photograph is of my great-grandfather removing railings from All Saints' Church, Maidstone. The year was July 1941. The railings were melted down to provide iron for guns and tanks, used in the Second World War. The photograph was taken by the *Kent Messenger* and published. The photograph holds great personal value to my family as shortly after it was taken unfortunately my great grandfather died, but I know a lot about him. His name was Charles Eiffert, and he fought in the First World War in the Royal Horse Artillery where he received two medals. He was very brave. (Lindsay Rogers, St Simon Stock School)

This is my husband's grandfather, James McHardy, born in Crathes, Scotland, in 1836. When James reached the age of 14, he wanted to join a Highland Regiment to fight in the Crimean War in 1850. Being only 14, he lied about his age to join up. The photograph was taken in about 1853 when he would have been 17. He had already won three stripes. When the war was over, he returned to farming in the Highlands. (Gabrielle McHardy)

My mother Annetta and her parents Henrietta and George Williamson, members of the Edinburgh and Leith Shetland Association (which the latter had founded) at the Leith Pageant in about 1930. George, a much respected activist in the labour and co-operative movements during the first half of the century, stood as a Labour candidate for Gorgie Ward. He also ran a successful accountancy business and it was said that he charged his clients according to their means for his services. I wonder how many socialists today would adopt such idealistic principles. (Beverley Wright)

Thomas Penrose was born in Leigh, Lancashire, and was educated at Leigh Parish School. On 16 January 1908, he married Edith Morris and they had four children – Alice, Lizzie, Edith and Tom. He joined the Army in the First World War as Pte 24616 of the South Wales Borderers and while being transported to Gallipoli on the ship *Royal Edward* it was sunk on 15 August 1915. He spent five hours in the water on a barrel before he was rescued. Here he is enjoying his pipe shortly before he died in 1961. (Barry Carman)

This is my great-great-uncle Lambert as a choir boy at the age of 9. He sang at St George's Methodist Church, which has now been demolished and replaced with bungalows. When Lambert was 19, he joined the Army as a despatch rider but on 12 October 1940, he was travelling through London when an army lorry collided with him and he died at the age of 23. (Emma Pilling)

This is a picture of my daddy, Livingstone Augustus Burke. The *Windrush* of 1945 paved the way for many West Indians to come to 'the land of milk and honey'. He arrived in 1955 then sent for my mother, Louise May Rowe, to join him in 1956. They were soon married. My parents found the changes hard. No jobs, no one would rent them rooms. People were frightened and branded them 'coloureds'. My parents moved from town to town. They paved the way for my generation, my children's generation and the generations to come. (Cherry Theodore)

Grandma in her sitting room in High Street, Ogmore Vale, in the 1920s I believe. Her name was Margaret Raltnay and before her marriage she had been a teacher. She would have been quite at home today in my 34-year-old daughter's sitting room as some of her pieces are there. The pendulum does swing back and it is wonderful to think that what was enjoyed at the beginning of the century is being appreciated at its close. Hopefully, this will still be happening in the next millennium. (Margaret Williams)

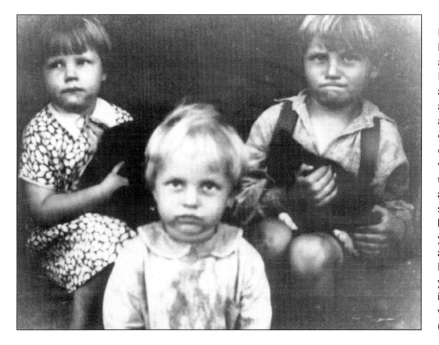

In about 1934 we were living in squalid conditions at the barracks in Folkestone. My father was a regular soldier and away a great deal of the time and I have vivid memories of mice sitting on the bed chewing things. Later, we were all taken away into the care of Dr Barnardo's and my three sisters separated from my brother and me for many years. Fortunately, my adult life was better and I now enjoy my happiest years as a pensioner living in Spain, but the scars will always be there. (Mr R.J.T. Daltry)

My grandmother was about 18 when this was taken. She was in service in North London learning to be a cook. Her 'young man' was a soldier, still in South Africa at the end of the Boer War. To have this portrait taken to send to him, all the 'downstairs' staff contributed and gave my grandmother her pick of their Sunday Best outfits so that she would look her finest. (Sue Osborne)

This photograph is of my two brothers, William Crocker and Thomas Crocker. Both died in the Spanish flu outbreak at the end of the First World War. (Frank Crocker)

A photo like this was taken annually at Blackpool with the family who always went together, not being able to afford to go abroad (unthinkable then!). We looked forward to this holiday annually after my hardworking parents saved up faithfully for me and my sister's benefit. My parents always entered me in 'Uncle Peter's Talent Show' which I usually won from the age of 6 and I am still in show business! The family always came first and stuck together, out of love and respect, important issues in those times. (Pamela Shaw)

This picture was taken inside the Stag Inn at Barkston, Lincolnshire, c. 1912. It shows the landlord, my great-grandfather, and great-grandmother, Mr and Mrs George Blackbourn, together with their parrot and dogs. Behind is a grapevine which, I understand, was a feature in the pub. Their son, James Blackbourn, was killed during the First World War and his name is recorded on the village war memorial. Their daughter, Dinah, was my grandmother. We visited the pub in 1989 and to that day, a small part of the vine, together with the parrots and dogs, was still a feature. (John Roberts)

A photo of our Dad, Otis Manasseh Orteseh, from Edinburgh. He is the first ever Orteseh in Britain. A former naval marine engineer officer, he was born in Gboko, Nigeria, in 1949 and joined the Royal Navy at HMS *Fisgard* in 1970 through the Commonwealth exchange scheme. He is a dual citizen of both Britain and Nigeria. He is also a local actor, singer and radio/club DJ. His pictures were part of the Edinburgh multicultural city arts exhibition in October 1996 to January 1997. His dream is to be famous one day. (Kim and Donna Orteseh)

Mrs Johanna Davey, photographed on her 90th birthday in 1997, is holding a catalogue for an exhibition of the works of Irish artist William J. Leech (1881–1968). It is open at a painting of herself by the artist in 1937, loaned by her at the time for the exhibition shown in Dublin and London. As Johanna Wirz, she came to England in 1935 from her native Switzerland and became a governess, teaching German to Princesses Elizabeth (our present Queen) and Margaret, at Windsor during the war. She still lives in Hampton after more than sixty years. (John Davey)

This photograph of my mother posing with the archery team was taken in 1959 at Stoke Mandeville Hospital where she stayed for several years after having both legs amputated. My mother travelled from South Shields to receive treatment at Stoke Mandeville, a revolutionary hospital in its time. It enabled her to learn to walk with prosthetics and to generally become more independent. She died in 1994 aged 58, but I will always remember how courageous and kind she was, and I know part of her lives on in me. (Karen Manning)

This is us – the Jheeta family, from Punjab, India. My name is Sohan, my younger brother, Ranjit and my mother Surjit. We arrived in this country in August 1964. We have called England our home and represent as much British way of life as any other British person. My mother is wearing traditional Indian dress. My brother and I are sporting the height of 1972 fashion. I wore grey bell-bottoms, fluorescent eau-de-nil jacket with black velvet pockets and a purple necktie. I sported a Dave Hill (of Slade) hairdo. (Sohan Jheeta)

This photograph, taken on Waxham Beach, Norfolk, in 1993, shows my son Louis, then aged 2, seeking some cool refreshment. As a parent, it can be a constant worry that your children's diet may not be as pure as it could be. The latter part of the century has been a time of many health scares over various foods and drinks. With several scares concerning meat, perhaps it is not surprising that vegetarianism is on the increase, but it is difficult to avoid the many additives in foods today and what of the GM foods of tomorrow? (Joanna Rice)

This is my father, photographed at Fort George in 1940 when he was a Seaforth Highlander. Very apt for someone from Manchester! Taken after the sacrifice of the 51 Highland Division at St Valery, he was wounded but, with three companions, stole a staff car reaching the port of La Baule near St Nazaire and escaping to England on a destroyer. He was sent home on leave, and appeared in court and fined 2s after being involved in a scuffle with his younger brother who jokingly said he wore a skirt. He died in 1992. (Albert John Tasker)

My grandparents on their wedding day on 18 June 1919. They were married at the Zion Chapel in Hulme, Manchester (this is now part of the Hulme revival and used as an arts centre). The picture was probably taken with a plate camera and it is likely that they would have been asked to stand still for at least one minute. (Jacqui Ellis)

This is my parents' wedding day. The photo was taken outside the village institute, the corrugated-iron building in the background, with the Home Guard. The village institute was like a working men's club, built for recreational purposes. The village is Boughton Manchelsea, 4 miles south-east of Maidstone in Kent. My father was a farm labourer and member of the local Home Guard. (Mary Jean Bowles)

A photo of my two daughters Rebecca (6) and Joanna (4), near Ide Hill in Kent during the summer of 1993. The picture captures the innocence of two small girls with their dolls outside the nurseries which bear their family surname. Maybe when they are married with a different surname, they will show their children this image of Bridge Nurseries. (Steve Bridge)

My two daughters and two of our famous runners of the century, Chris Chataway and Dr Roger Bannister at Lyminster in Sussex, in the summer of 1968. My daughters are now both teachers and married with children of their own, the younger one living in Australia and the elder one in Upminster, Essex. The photograph reminds me of a happy holiday and meeting two of the greatest sportsmen of the century. They were also two of the most charming gentlemen you could wish to meet. (Mrs J. Ayres)

This is a photo taken at Hungerford Road Infants School, Islington, in 1927. The class was oversized, with thirty-one children, including me. We were mostly very poor because of the depression, unemployment, and little or no benefits. But we had pride and burning ambition, were clean, polite, could read, write, spell and count. We were examined for literacy and numeracy twice a week. How many of these children are alive today? We paid our dues, fought and sacrificed for our country which now regards us as a burden to be sidelined and penalised for being old. Our pride has now been replaced by greed. (Mrs M.E. Cooke)

This picture was taken at the summit of Helvellyn in the Lake District in 1959 by my father, A.H. Sleigh. The picture is of my brother and myself, together with the family dog that pulled him up the mountain. Note the '50s style of dress and the Brownie 127 camera. Striding Edge is in the background. (John Sleigh)

Every picture tells a story. You'd say we look comfortable, but the reality was far from it. A tatty, damp, rented house, with no mod-cons. Treadling the sewing machine, I made our clothes while my husband biked 12 miles to work each day. Sunday afternoon walks in 1954 by the canal with putt-putting barges, my sons picking wild flowers for me, leave only sweet memories. I, being a war evacuated Londoner, loved the countryside, though I felt an outsider in a close-knit community of railway workers. Now I live in Milton Keynes, I'm back again in the city. (Mrs Doris E. White)

This photograph is of my father, Thomas Henry Bates, and was taken at a sitting at Eastern Studio in Singapore in 1924. I, born in Murree, India (now Pakistan) was then 1 year old. My brother, Edward, was born in Singapore in 1925. We were raised in Calcutta by our mother to believe 'daddy' had died. Only when she died in Nairobi in 1968 did we discover he had not died when we were toddlers. Since then I have been searching for him but, because of the break-up of the British Empire, the task now appears to be hopeless. (Thomas J. Bates)

I like this photo, it really captured the moment It shows my wife, Jane, and daughter Rebecca (on the left) concentrating on the task of making jam tarts, 1988. My son, who did not want to miss out on the event, was finding better things to do with the pastry. A valuable lesson in a traditional skill, when the microwave cooker was still a relatively new gadget in the kitchen. (Chris Goodacre)

I was 14 years old when I photographed my younger brother Eric, on the right, and cousin David during a trainspotting expedition we had at Haymarket Station, Edinburgh, in 1965. As well as capturing the last days of steam, this picture seems to sum up the end of an age of innocence when youngsters could travel around the country by themselves in relative safety. (Trevor Ermel)

This family photograph dates from the mid-1920s. The lady in the swimsuit is my late mother-in-law, Elizabeth Brown, the boy is her son Alfie who was killed in the war and the girl is her daughter, Queenie. The lady in the hat is Great-Aunt Kate who lived to be 96 and kept her false teeth in her pocket! The picture was taken in Northumberland and the car, an Austin 12/4, was the family's first. (Mrs Wendy Brown)

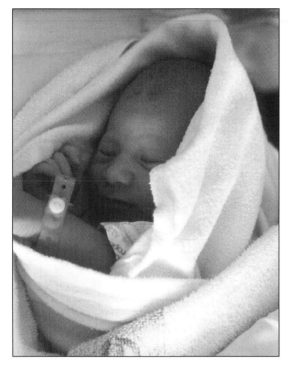

Stephen James Reid, born at 9.06 a.m. on 13 March 1996 at Leighton Hospital, Crewe. This was taken about an hour after Stephen's birth. Witnessing my son's arrival into the world was such an incredible experience. Until quite recently, it was almost unheard of for fathers to be present at the birth of their children, now it is commonplace. When I took this photo with such joy in my heart, I had no idea of the horrific events occurring in Dunblane. Later on I heard that sixteen schoolchildren and their teacher had been shot dead. (Malcolm Reid)

This photo is of our 3-year-old son Richard Peter Walker playing in the garden and posing with his sunglasses one sunny afternoon in July 1999 in Cardiff. This moment of Richard happy and smiling is special to us as two years ago he underwent treatment for cancer of the eyes and he has successfully come through the courses of chemotherapy and radiotherapy. He is a living example that cancer can be beaten. He is a happy, handsome, bright little boy who loves and lives life to the full – we are so very proud of him. (Susan K. Walker)

My mother and younger sister Camilla in 1960. They are on board the liner *Statendam*, returning to England from the United States where the family had spent the previous year. We lived in Minnesota and I attended the local school. I know that my parents often wondered if they should have stayed on in America, and perhaps this ambivalence about returning to chilly England shows in my mother's face. Although liners are now used for expensive cruises, at that time it was the normal way to travel to the States: flying was too expensive. (Rosamond Allwood)

This is my great-aunt, Carrie Bowden, who was born in 1903. She was one of nine children of whom only four survived childhood. She died in 1973. The photograph was taken at 29 Habershon Street, Splott, Cardiff, in September 1912 by her father who was a mason. Photography was his hobby. Carrie's mother, Mary Hanna Morgan, came from mid-Wales and was a seamstress who made Corpus Christi dresses for the children of Splott. The photograph reflects hard times when only basic facilities were available and when it was commonplace to see a 9-year-old girl peeling potatoes with a knife. (Geraldine Bousie)

My mother was born in 1905 and was 17 years old in this photograph which my father took with him out to the Argentine while in service. The picture was found in a box of crumpled and neglected photos. I loved the photo from the moment I saw it, mainly for its beauty and simplicity, just a teenager of the 1920s era. Now I want to take her and all her fine qualities with me into the new millennium; after all she is my past, present and future. (Mrs A. Godrey)

This photograph was taken at the International Model Railway Exhibition in 1988, which was opened by the Rev. W. Awdry. It shows on the left Christopher Awdry, the current writer and Rev. W Awdry, the creator of the Thomas the Tank Engine stories, the first story being written in 1943 for his son who had measles at the time. It is reckoned by the Awdry family, who know the photographer well, to be one of the best ones taken of the two people. (Allan C. Mott)

A photograph of my great-great-grandfather who worked on a farm in Norfolk: the dog walking alongside him is called Jet. He used to collect straw at harvest time and stack it up using a pitchfork. He had a range of animals including cows and sheep. If you look carefully you can see a house in the background. That is where my great-great-gran worked. He had five or six fields and the one in the background is his biggest. It is a shame that there are not more farms. (Rachel Beale, Henham and Ugley Primary School)

This was taken in Scarborough in 1946. It shows my sister on the left, and my late wife, Margaret, on the right. We were married on Christmas Eve 1945, shortly after which I was posted to Egypt for two years. They took the opportunity to gad about during a stint in Holland (there is a book full of pictures from that, including Nijmegen and Arnhem) and Youth Hostelling in this country. (Colin Reid)

My great-aunt Ivy, collecting water from the village pump. She lived in the village of Langtoft, East Yorkshire, and all the water had to be carried home in buckets in the days before water was pumped directly to the houses. (Ashley Cowton, Headlands School)

My grandfather on his summer holidays in 1933. In every picture we have of him he is wearing his bowler hat. In those days a gentleman would not be considered properly dressed without a hat. He is even wearing it here on the beach at Brighton. I wonder what he would think of today's topless bathing! (Janet Dodson)

This is a picture of me and my father in the early 1930s. It is significant to me because there is nothing more traditional to this nation than the game of cricket, and my father left us shortly after the picture was taken. I never saw him again until his death at around 90 years of age. (Gordon Dean)

A photograph taken in 1938 by my father, using a Box Brownie camera. We were on a family day out to Southampton to see the ocean-going liners and the New Forest ponies on the way home. Pre-war Southampton was the UK terminus for all worldwide travel. After the war, when people could take holidays again, air travel offered a cheaper and quicker way to reach their destination. (Mrs B. Stiddard)

My great-grandparents outside their new home, a farm in Ainsdale (Southport), to which they moved from Burnley in 1904. The photo is serene, has a country feel, and depicts more fortunate working-class people at the start of this century. It shows too that there was some movement of families even then. Their name was Bradshaw, and the lane to their farm is Bradshaw's Lane. The farm has now gone. (Mrs Evelyn Atkins)

This is a copy of a much-faded wedding photo. My brother and I acted as pages to our cousin Bert and his bride in 1929. Standing at the back left is Uncle Richard with his wife, Sarah. (Colin Reid)

Our family in the school hall of St Matthew's Junior and Infants, September 1998. In the photograph are me, my partner, our two sons and daughter. Looking at our children, you can see very much the changing face of Britain today. Our children are of mixed parentage and while this is not acceptable to many parts of this society, we try to teach our children the importance of their shared cultures. We also teach them pride in themselves and to respect every person they meet regardless of skin colour, creed, race or religion, because we are all human beings. (Veronica Gayle)

This, I think, reflects the way many people choose to get married. The photograph of my sister and brother-in-law was taken in a more informal environment – in a register office. After this photo was taken, my sister and brother-in-law flew off abroad. I think that instead of having a traditional more expensive wedding, people give more thought to their honeymoon. Apart from that, there have been more remarriages and after people have been married once, they settle for a smaller wedding the second time round. Besides, if they have children from previous marriages, it would seem more practical and economical to have a smaller wedding. (Victoria Grundy)

work

I live in East Kilbride, a very modern town with shopping malls and lots of entertainment. My life is full of gadgets. The motor car plays a major part in our lives. This picture shows my grandfather's family in approximately 1930 working at hay making. It shows how different life was then. The men are wearing shirts and waistcoats, they are using simple tools and the plough was pulled by a Clydesdale. It reminds us that there was a time when power came from ways that did less damage to the environment. (Fiona Weir, Duncanrig Secondary School, **Secondary School Winner**)

This is a photograph of my dad, taken in around 1965 at All Saints' Church, Reading, kissing the bride. It was traditional for a chimney sweep to be present after the wedding. It represented a token of good luck. This is now a rare sight. Dad took a lot of pride in his work, so I wanted to share this and give people the opportunity of knowing this, because my dad was very precious to me, and I was very proud of him, sooty or not! (Avril Ward)

This photograph, which was taken in 1928 at Waverley Station, Edinburgh, is of my great-great-grandfather standing on the famous steam train the *Flying Scotsman* 4472. His name was Thomas Roper (far left of the picture), nicknamed 'Hellfire Tom'. He was one of the drivers on the non-stop train journey from Edinburgh to Kings Cross, London. This photograph is of value both personally and historically as this event was one of the great moments in the history of transport and will always be of interest to people who are enthusiastic about steam trains. (Gillian Eunson, Preston Lodge High School, **Secondary School Winner**)

A photo taken in the 1920s of my great-grandad, Harry Penny, standing outside the mines after an explosion in the coal pit with a dead canary because he was using the canary to see if there would be an explosion. It died showing the gases were high and there was an explosion. His best friend died in the disaster. It all happened in Ebbw Vale. (Alex Grady, Reigate Grammar, **Secondary School Winner**)

This photograph, taken in the 1930s, is of my great-great-grandfather William Thickett, shown on the far left, working on the gargoyles of a local church. It is of personal value because he was a relation of mine and because it has been passed down through the family. William was born in 1856, the son of a Horbury builder, and lived most of his life in Wakefield. Early in his life he learned the trade of stone masonry and during his long working career he was involved in such projects as the restoring of Wakefield Cathedral, the building of the Divisional Police Headquarters in Wood Street and the Municipal Baths in Sun Lane. For the last twenty-four years of his career he was a foreman bricklayer working for George Crook & Sons, supervising young apprentices and workers alike. He died in 1945 at the age of 88. (Richard Mathewman, St Wilfrids CE High School, **Secondary School Winner**)

This photo shows us what supermarkets were like in 1954. My grandma is advertising Naafi Tea. It shows us all different products, e.g. Cadbury's drinking chocolate, Rice, Creamola, Nestlé instant coffee and Carnation milk. They are only some of the products. As you can see my grandma is wearing a small hat, some pearls, a pair of small gloves, a jacket, a long skirt and she has her hair in a bob. The shopkeeper is wearing a long overall and his hair gelled back. (Nicola Giles, Tolworth Girls' School, **Secondary School Winner**)

Zachariah Pritchard was my great-grandfather; he was born in 1874 in the Rhondda Valley. After fighting in the First World War he was demobilised with a piece of shrapnel near his heart. He became a chimney sweep – a good job because most people burnt coal to keep warm and the soot needed to be swept from the chimney. His brushes can be seen in the photo and his face is black from soot. During a violent coughing fit, due to bronchitis, the shrapnel moved to his heart and he died aged 64. This photo is important because sweeps are becoming rarer at the end of the twentieth century. (Simon Phipps, Willowfield School, **Secondary School Winner**)

Grain farmers in Lincolnshire traditionally burned the stubble late every summer after the harvest. By the 1970s, the thick smoke and black ash was so bad, filling houses and causing road accidents because of the poor visibility, that stubble burning was made illegal. I took this photo in the mid-1980s in one of the last years of this historic practice. (Roger Minshull, **Runner Up**)

This picture was taken by my grandfather. He told me stories of when he was in the Air Force. He joined the Air Force many years before the start of the Second World War and worked in India when it was part of the British Empire. He navigated the plane. It must have been dangerous. He took this photograph of the Himalayas from his plane. The picture is interesting because of the different parts of history in one place, the early Air Force, the British Empire, the old planes and the Himalayas, which no one had really visited at that time. (Matthew Moran, **Winner**)

This is a photograph of my grandfather (second from the right) taken in the first few years of the century. Although mechanisation was taking place on farms, crops were still cut by hand using teams of men with scythes. This was a very hard, laborious and skilful task. Today, large areas can be cut by one man on a combine-harvester. My grandfather was born in Norfolk but had to move to Devon and then Kent to find work. It is believed the photograph was taken in Kent. (B.J. Saunders, **Winner**)

The very last of the Midlands horse-drawn narrow boats which ended its working life removing waste matter from a West Bromwich factory. Here it is going through the coal boat offloading area of the Ocker Hill power station built in 1902 and thought then to be the largest in the country. At its peak, the power station was burning half a million tons of coal per year. It was closed in 1977. (Mr E.C. Smith, **Runner Up**)

This photo was taken of my uncle, David Vaughan, in his workshop at Alderley Edge in Cheshire in 1990. He was a cabinet maker and antiques restorer from the 1930s to the '90s: more than sixty years in all, with a six-year break while fighting in the Second World War. Here he is working on a Georgian corner cabinet. He had a wonderful unique collection of carpentry tools covering many decades. His work was his life and the quality of his craftsmanship and the lifetime's dedication to his trade is becoming a rarity today. (Anita Brown, **Winner**)

My grandfather, on a hay cart in the 1920s, loading the hay on the device driven by the pony on the right walking in circles. My grandfather, Mr William Hall, was working at Acreland Farm, Grafton Underwood on the Duke of Buccleuch's Estate, near Kettering. (Mrs Freda Sheppard, **Runner Up**)

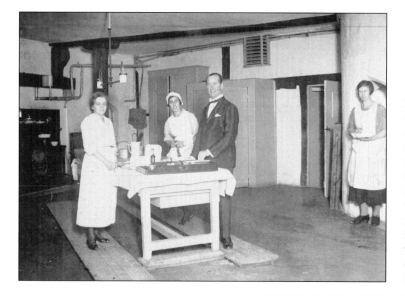

My grandmother (left) was cook at Walmer Castle in the late 1920s with a housemaid and scullery maid under her. The smiling gentleman is the butler. Life 'below stairs' was not luxurious: the boards were because the floor was cold to stand on, cooking was on the coal range in the background and the whole building was gas lit at the time. It took my grandmother a long time to really appreciate electric lighting. She was a superb cook and could make light sponge cakes without the aid of the electric mixers now considered indispensable. (Sue Osborne, **Runner Up**)

My aunt (far right) when she was working in service at a country house in Caerphilly, South Wales, in 1916. In those days, after leaving school, girls from a working-class family either found employment in service or as shop assistants. My aunt's day would start at 6 a.m. and her working day would end at 7 p.m. with one afternoon off a week. However, she had many happy memories of her years in service. The domestic staff who always lived in were just like her second family. (Gwyneth Birkenshaw, **Winner**)

Alice Harris died in 1970, aged 100. She was one of the first to use photographs (lantern slides) for human rights campaigning. Here she is pictured with a group of African children, c. 1904 (photograph from the Harris collection at the Anti-Slavery Library). Alice went to the Belgian Congo with her missionary husband John in 1900 where she collected extensive photographic evidence of atrocities perpetrated upon indigenous rubber workers and their families. On returning to England, Alice and her husband toured the country giving illustrated lectures on the situation in the Congo, using Alice's lantern slides. (Rebecca Smaga, **Runner Up**)

This is a picture of my father, long deceased, 'mushing' out of Paddington, Marylebone and Bayswater in 1905. 'Mushing' in cabbies' language meant getting a cab on hire purchase and working every hour possible to keep up the payments. Leonard Cottrell, at 15 years of age and a member of a distinguished family of coaching people, was given full responsibility for their one horseless carriage. He is seen here between jobs outside the family home in the Mews off Seymour Street and within a stone's throw of Marble Arch. Alec Cottrell, **Runner Up**)

This is a photograph I took of George Massey, a chimney sweep from Stoke-on-Trent. George was 81 years old when this photograph was taken in May 1997 and he was still working an average of forty hours a week. George is one of that dying breed of self-employed people whose job has been diminished by advances in clean air, closure of the coal pits and greater environmental expectations of a new age. George says he likes his job a lot but might retire when he gets to 90! (Lindsay Heywood, **Runner Up**)

My father, Fred Shires, in 1961 at his work in Oldham. He was a skip maker, a highly skilled tradesman. A skip is a large rectangular open basket, woven out of thick cane and was used intensively in the old cotton mills for carrying the cotton from one process to the next. Sadly, because of the advent of cheaper materials and the decline of the cotton industry they are no longer in use. Working conditions were very spartan, without heating or comfort, and extremely harsh in winter. (Mrs Doris Harrison, **Runner Up**)

In these days of controversy over tobacco smoking, this photo shows my late mother Rose Lovering working in the 1920s at Wills Woodbine Factory in Bristol. All cigarettes were hand-rolled as there was no machinery then. My mother (third from the left) is being overlooked by the late George VI and could roll two cigarettes one in each hand, despite never having smoked in her life. Also in the frame is Queen Elizabeth, the Queen Mother. If one day in the future tobacco is outlawed, you will never again have photos such as this to look back on. Mrs Maureen Epton, **The Express Runner Up**)

This photo was taken in 1971 in Horley, Surrey, and shows an era when knife grinders called at houses to sharpen kitchen and garden equipment. (Tony Boxall, **Runner Up**)

At Leigh-on-Sea commercial cockle fishing and shrimping has gone on for hundreds of years. Until recently the cockle beds were raked, the cockles gathered into large wicker baskets and, using a yoke, were carried to the cockle boat and emptied into the hold after which they were removed by the same basket method and cooked prior to selling. Now large suction hoses are used and it is said that the beds will be ruined as the suction hoses take up not only the mature cockles but the immature ones as well. The hand method of gathering will never be seen again in the Thames Estuary. (Roy Smith, **Runner Up**)

A school photo taken in 1931. My aunt, aged 8, is in the back row. Boys and girls were taught separately in large classes. The pupils sat at double desks with combined seats. Inkwells were filled each day by ink monitors. Pupils had to sit up straight and hands were out of sight except when writing. None of the children's work is on display and the classroom is very drab and formal compared with today's schools. (Beverley Reynolds, **Runner Up**)

This snap of my mother-in-law was taken in 1933 by the butler with his box camera. Mary was working as a domestic at the time and her athletic carpet sweeping must have helped to keep her fit as she lived to be 101 years old. Hard work and low pay was the lot of the servant in those days but, as can be seen from the photo, they still managed to find time for a little fun. Mary Miles was a jolly lady who came up smiling despite hard times and two world wars, and we all miss her. (Mrs June Miles, **Runner Up**)

Villages in County Durham sprang up around colliery sites. Terraces were provided to house the miners and their families. At Blackhall, terraced streets took the names of the rows, Sixth Street, Seventh Street, etc., while the colliery sat at the bottom of the avenues, a few hundred yards away. Coal hewing was a hard, dirty job and at that time the mainstay of the North East; every village would hear the clatter of the pit winding gear and wagons. Here, miners come off shift at Blackhall in 1974. (Ray Kitching, **Runner Up**)

This photograph, taken in 1911, shows my late mother Minnie Hunter. My grandfather was headmaster at this Gloucestershire school, Berkeley Senior Council School – the first purpose-built experimental school in a purely agricultural area. The staff consisted of the head, two male and two female teachers with visiting staff for metalwork, woodwork and housewifery. Livestock was kept – hens, ducks, pigs, bees and rabbits. Different rooms were fitted with practical gadgets – tools, lathes, forges, saws, etc. When the First World War broke out, male staff and pupil teachers enlisted. The school eventually became a primary school. It was a forerunner of future technical education. (Janet A. Stevenson, **Runner Up**)

My father, Herbert 'Bert' Pitts, working for Pritchards, a bakery in Muswell Hill in the early 1930s. Anyone familiar with the hilly nature of Muswell Hill area will realise that pulling a laden cart would be very hard work. Pritchards also owned a function room, for which my father would act as caretaker and also play the piano accordion in the band. I think it's interesting that in the 1930s Pritchards style themselves 'electric machine bakeries', proud of modern techniques, whereas now manufacturers emphasise how natural and traditional their products are. (Norman Pitts, **Winner**)

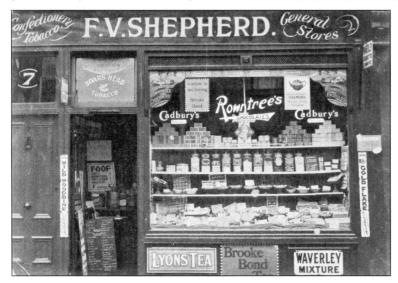

My grandmother's shop in Islington photographed in 1932. She sold sweets, cigarettes, patent medicines and ointments and dry goods such as tea, sugar, cocoa, etc. She made her own ice cream and toffee apples and sold drinks by the glass, hot in winter, cold in summer. The shop was open until 10 p.m. and the local youngsters, including myself, gathered there to play her pinball machine and chat. My grandmother kept the shop until she was in her 70s and died in 1969 at the age of 90. The shop would not survive today. (Ann Pienkos, **Runner Up**)

This photo is of an incident which will never be forgotten – the Remembrance Day bombing by the IRA of Enniskillen in 1987. I was a Corporal in the Royal Irish Rangers photographing suspect cars and people when the explosion occurred. NO newspapers in Ireland or England got wind of these photos and I don't wish them to without my permission. Twelve innocent people died, paying their respects to the men and women who granted us freedom during the First World War. They gave their tomorrows so that we can live today. The bronze statue tells it all. (John Corrigan, **Runner Up**)

The shepherd in the picture is Ronnie Morland. Until his retirement a few years ago, he used to work the slopes of Criffel which, at just under 2000 ft, is the highest hill in Dumfriesshire. Despite the rugged and steep terrain, he never used motorised buggies. He walked everywhere, some days from dawn to dusk. For such a big man, it was a pleasure to witness the way that he looked after the new lambs in his care. In these intensive farming days, it would be reassuring to know that Ronnie's traditional ways are still being practised. (Derek Ross, **Runner Up**)

This photograph captures an old friend in a situation quite alien to our friendship, depicting her at work. Personally it is of significance because of our friendship, but also because of her achievements within her industry. In this way, it becomes historically significant depicting the rise of women in industry, something unheard of until this century. For future generations it will probably signify outdated modes of manufacturing, but hopefully it will contribute to their understanding of twentieth-century society. (Rebekah Good, **Runner Up**)

Left: This picture won first prize of 2 guineas in a 'Happy Snapshot' competition in our local newspaper in 1955. Local children loved to 'help' at Leap Mill Farm at Burnopfield in Co. Durham and Ben Turnbull, the farmer, tolerated us remarkably well as he ran the farm largely single-handed. We had watched the pikes of hay being pulled on to the pike bogie by chains. We then jumped on for the ride from the field to the farm. The farmer has his arm around my shoulder. This was an old-fashioned scene even then because of increasing mechanisation. (Dorothy Rand, **Runner Up**)

Right: My grandfather's eldest brother Sidney, standing in the doorway of the family home and shop in Gillingham, Dorset, with a fine crab in his hand, 1913. A year later, his six younger brothers went off to fight in the First World War. Two were killed in action on the Somme and at Ypres, and Great-Uncle Percy lost an arm and an eye. Sidney's sisters were put into service with local wealthy families and by the 1920s all the remaining children had left the business and my grandfather became a school caretaker. The Gillingham business still survives as a family concern but now as a small supermarket. (Jim Kite, **Winner**)

Left: My father (a brickwork contractor) and his gang of bricklayers and labourers in about 1903. The building they were working on was in Petty France and was to be the tallest in London. In the early years of the twentieth century the Underground was being constructed. There were a number of settlements occurring in existing buildings close to the lines of the new railways. Petty France suffered a number of such faults and when the building in this photograph reached first floor level, the project was halted and did not continue for a number of years and then to a reduced height. (Joan Syrett, **Winner**)

Right: My grandad, Sidney William Stead (second from the right), at the LNER offices in York, 1940s. It was from here in May and early June 1944 that he helped to organise trains taking troops to the south coast for the D-Day landings. So many soldiers were on the move that some had to march south until he could get a train to pick them up at a convenient station. Note the card index system controlling the movement of trains – this was long before computerisation which many of us now take for granted. (Zoë Stead, **Runner Up**)

My grandad in 1987. He was competing in the Master Upholsterers' Competition at the Kent County Show Ground in Detling. It has significant value for the future because in the future, most crafts like upholstering may not survive because of the advance in technology. Soon it will die out as there is little interest in it as a future job and machines will take over the work. This photo has significant value to me too, as not many people I know have a relation that knows and uses such a craft. (Andrew Franklin, Ringmer Community College)

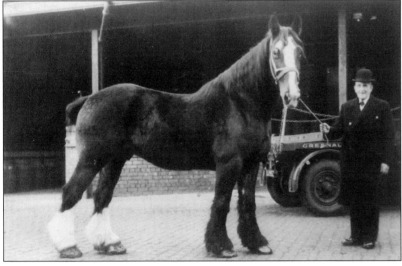

Grandfather worked from the age of 10 until the day he died in 1948, at the age of 86. His happiest years spanned two decades when he was solely responsible for the welfare and training of the teams of Shires which pulled the brewery drays. He is saying goodbye to Prince, his final charge. The new lorries wait. Mechanisation has taken over and the old man is to be yard foreman, spending his last few years checking the lorries in and out of this yard. This picture and all Prince's burnished brasses have pride of place in our home. (Margaret Richardson)

This photo is of interest to me because it marks the demise of a village brewery at Leeming Bar, North Yorks. The photo was taken at its closure in 1926 which caused a lot of unemployment in that village. This was Plew's Brewery and it closed because it was becoming possible to make better beers that lasted longer and could travel further and not spoil, and village breweries were not needed. Once every village made its own beers. Most of these men have at least a handsome moustache and a good flat cap. (David Howlett, St Teresa's RC Primary School)

This is the re-enactment of my school's official opening in December 1998. My Headteacher, P. Phillips Esq., is shaking hands with one of the haberdashers, Mr M. Wheldon. Our MP, Mr P. Murphy, is there with Sir Richard Hanbury-Tennyson and some of the school governors. My brother, Owen, is one of the boys in Victorian dress. When the school opened it was for boys only. This is my last year and I am Head Boy. I wonder who will be Head Boy in 2098 when the school celebrates its second centenary. (Rhys Miller, West Monmouth School)

This picture was taken in Rokeby Road, Brockley, south-east London, at Easter 1982. From left to right are Susan Nicol, and me, the mother-in-law, Ruth Nicol. We are following the trend of the 1980s to DIY. The photographer is Keith Nicol, marking the start of their new kitchen and bathroom extension. When the time came to lay the concrete floor, one of my other sons, Christopher, lost his watch, which must now be buried under Keith and Susan's kitchen floor. Happy days! Women's Lib wields the sledgehammer, it says it all. (Mrs Ruth Nicol)

My grandad in 1942 when he began work as an apprentice in a factory which made gas fittings. He started this job when he was 17, part time, to earn some money, but ended up using his skills in this trade to open a dry cleaners, which was the family business for twenty years. My grandad's friends helped him to set up the shop, using spare pipes as railings in the windows to store the clothes, and my grandad did all the fittings himself. He died at the age of 60 in 1988. (Jenny Graham, Howard of Effingham School)

We will never see these prices again. This is in 1934 in Newcastle-upon-Tyne. I was 17 years old, the tallest young man was my boyfriend, 21 years old and manager of the shop. Two years later he was called up for the Second World War serving as a Desert Rat in Tobruk and a Chindit in Burma. He survived to work for a large food group and retired as General Manager. Our golden wedding was in 1990. (Ellen Brew)

A photograph taken in May 1991 of my parents Grace and Charles Wood at the entrance to the Geevor Tin Mine, Land's End, Cornwall. The mine had recently closed and they were allowing visitors to go down the mine shaft and walk through the workings which extended right under the Atlantic Ocean. The mining company was keeping the pumps going in the hope that a buyer could be found. Unfortunately, none was forthcoming and in consequence the mine was allowed to flood in September 1991, ending many years of tin mining in the area. (Glynis Wood)

This is a photo of Tim, me (Danny), Nathan and Mark. The picture was taken on 25 July 1994 while on 5 Airborne Brigade Exercise, Pegasus Strike. Just after this photo was taken, we were told that we were to fly out to Rwanda in forty-eight hours to provide humanitarian aid for up to 500,000 refugees. We were in Rwanda for four months and achieved a great deal of satisfaction while we were out there. This photo is special to me since when we returned, we were posted to different parts of the UK and very rarely see each other. (Danny Benton)

My dad in the middle, my younger brother Rich on the quad bike and my cousin James. My dad is a sheep farmer and has had the quad bike for about ten years now. It has transformed his work especially at lambing time. James is also a sheep farmer. Although they have to work hard at certain times, they always seem to have time for a chat. (Judy Irving)

Infants, well into a cookery class in Barnby Road Primary, Newark, in 1985. This was in an old Victorian built school in an area of *Coronation Street* type homes of brick terraced back-to-back houses near to the town centre. Most photos in schools are of posed groups and special events like Sports Day. This is just a normal class on an ordinary day, sleeves up and hands on. (Roger Minshull)

Just before Christmas 1993 the train I was travelling on to work came to an abrupt halt. After nearly an hour at a standstill, we were instructed to climb down on to the track which had been switched off and walk back to Peckham BR station. London Underground and British Rail evacuated over 200,000 commuters after a series of warnings from the IRA, in spite of an historic Anglo-Irish peace accord the week before. (Gil Murray)

My uncle, Geoffrey Meynell. He is lifting his first bale of organically grown hay from his very first harvest in 1991. Organic farming has grown a lot in recent years as the number of people wanting to buy organic produce has increased. Concern for the environment will, I hope, be the main issue of the twenty-first century. (Jack Plant)

My mother, Grace Foskett, learned shorthand and typing at school. On leaving in 1926, she went to work in the advertising department of the LNER at Marylebone. With pencil at the ready, she would answer the boss's summons and take down, in shorthand, the letters he dictated before returning to the typist's room to transcribe them. Later, she would return with a sheaf of neatly typed letters for his signature. When she married in 1938, she left her job, as was normal; she never understood why I continued to work after I married. (Mary J. Morris)

This photograph was taken in 1932 and shows the office of the Continental Section, London North Eastern Railway Advertising Department at Marylebone, where I started work in 1930 at the age of eighteen. I am the lowly clerk on the left while Miss Robinson, the shorthand typist, is waiting for Mr Wheatley to finish his telephone conversation. Notice the contrast between the Head of Section's desk and the clerk's, symptomatic of our relative positions in the strict office hierarchy. The photograph was taken on my camera but I am not sure who pressed the shutter. (E.E. Burgis)

This is a photo of my grandfather William Ward, third row, second on the left, taken in 1902. He was a farmer from Middle Newton farm and later Newlands Farm, Cardiff. He had milk rounds in the Cardiff area and in those days the milk was in churns and delivered by horse and cart. How things have changed in this age. (Gordon Tanner)

As the twentieth century draws to a close, here is a scene at Drumcree Church, which could have come straight from the First World War: rows of trenches, ploughed fields, barbed and razor wire erected by the security forces to implement a Parades Commission ruling. The Orange Order was prevented from parading down the nationalist Garvaghy Road on the outskirts of Portadown. After a peaceful demonstration at the barricade, they re-routed their march and the day passed off without incident. (Mr S. Wilkinson)

Taken in 1960, this photo shows my father with some of his colleagues inside the offices of the BBC in Accra, Ghana. Dad, a journalist with the BBC World Service, was posted to this West African country in order to report on developments as it headed towards independence from Britain. This photo reflects a bygone era of office life in the British colonies and, looking at the cumbersome manual typewriter, also demonstrates how office technology has moved on. In a century punctuated by racial conflicts world wide, it is refreshing to see different races working harmoniously side by side. (Mrs Christina Sage)

My great-grandfather, Charles Mitchener (1849–1929), when he retired from his job as a tollkeeper on the South Parade Pier, in Southsea in 1919. The pier was opened in 1908 and survived until 1974 when it was destroyed by fire during the filming of Ken Russell's *Tommy*. When he retired he was presented with an onyx clock which was so heavy he had to take it home in a wheelbarrow. (Michael Bedford)

This is a photograph of the factory girls, taken on the steps of Dobson and Crowthers Paper Bag Manufacturers in Aston Road North. Note the turbans hiding the curlers, in for the 'big night out': quite a popular headgear in the early 1950s. This picture was taken in 1951, when I was 20 years old. (Violet Hoare)

My uncle Edwin Griffiths, sitting on his motor mower in the grounds of Ellesmere College, a boarding school for boys in Shropshire, 1932. He worked as a groundsman, taking care of the school grounds. He used to cycle 3 miles to work morning and night in all weathers until he retired in 1971 at the age of 77 after completing almost fifty years at the school. On his retirement, the headmaster presented him with a cheque in recognition of his long service. (C.K. Davies)

I took this picture one evening in 1966 at the patent shaft works in Wednesbury. It was one of the numerous iron and steel works on our doorstep. As a small group of office workers privileged to visit the foundry, we had an unforgettable insight into the heavy industry for which our area, known as the Black Country, was noted. The foundries have since been demolished. (Mrs K.M. Smith)

My great-grandmother, Catherine Mary Williams, standing outside her hat shop in Commercial Street, Aberdare, 1930. With her is her mother, Sarah King. Catherine was a trained milliner and after her husband died, aged 30, in 1925, she opened the shop to earn a living for herself and her daughter. (Madeline Williams)

My mother took this photograph of the girl who helped with the washing in the 1930s. Even though progress had been made from the poss tub it was still hard physical work. The agitator on this Ewbank washer was activated by vigorously turning the handle as shown here; more elbow grease was needed to turn the wringer. Washday was just that – a whole day devoted to washing and associated activities. Modern detergents and automatic washing machines save our energy and give us time for more interesting activities. (Dorothy Rand)

The lady in the foreground is my Auntie Irene. She is sorting through the Roses chocolates at the Cadbury factory in Bournville in 1947. The employees were allowed to eat as many chocolates as they wanted. This photo shows a visit by a French delegation sampling the chocolates at a time when luxuries such as these were still being rationed. (Kerry Phillips)

This photograph of my husband was taken thirty years ago, when he was base commander at Stonnington in the Antarctic as part of the British Antarctic Survey. Graham loved the splendour of isolation so much that he spent over six years in the frozen wastes. This picture is unique and it was the last time that dogs were used for transport: all of the dogs were shot when the survey left. They all had names and when out in the field, as Graham is here, your life literally depended on them. (Mrs G. Wright)

This was taken at the company I served my apprenticeship with, Smart and Brown (Engs) Ltd of Spennymoor, Co. Durham. It is a self-portrait taken when I was 21 years old and working as a draughtsman in the special purpose machine design office. Note the drawing board and equipment used (pencils etc.), no computers then. The company was part of the Thorn Group making light fittings, electric cookers, fridges and Ferguson televisions. This factory was in the old Royal Ordnance Buildings and was very basic. The company employed about 7,000 people from distances up to 15 miles away using buses, cars, motor and pedal cycles to get there. Plenty of work and jobs. My first wage was 47s for forty-five hours' work. (A. Wright)

This picture shows new horses undergoing noise rehearsals at Knightsbridge Barracks prior to the Coronation in June 1953. As it was the first Coronation since 1936 and the first of a Queen since Queen Elizabeth I in 1558, it was felt that a full Sovereign's Escort, not seen since the Second World War, should be mounted. There were insufficient horses and new ones, not trained for ceremonial duties, were pressed into service. Part of their acclimatisation was to have a lot of noise and waving of cloth of all descriptions, to try to get them ready for the Coronation. The training was a success. (Roy S. Smith)

From service in the trenches to service at the 'big house'. John Whittaker was my grandfather. He is pictured with other staff outside the house in Sutton Coldfield where he was a gardener after the First World War. As the century comes to a close his grandchildren and great-grandchildren are reaping the benefits of sweeping social change. John's chance of travel grew out of global conflict, employment was limited by a lack of educational opportunity. His descendants now aspire to university, the professions and travel in a continent at peace with itself. (Mrs K.M. Cronin)

This is a photo of my friend Ted. He works as a market trader in Brighton. As well as being a 'wheeler dealer', he is famous locally as a model for painting classes. He is with a life size portrait – the women in the background are borrowed from a famous Picasso picture. (Wendy Abbott)

This photograph was taken in the workshop of a cooper in the Burslem area of Stoke-on-Trent in the early 1980s. He was the last barrel maker in the potteries. As demand was low, he was to retire early and he was sad that the art of coopering was dying. (E.P. Bailey)

Outside Chichester Carphone Warehouse. My son Andrew, the Manager (left), and his Assistant Manager (right) have worked hard to make this one of the south's best-known communication centres. Mobile phones have become a way of life and, love them or loathe them, things will never be the same again. (Richard Cooke)

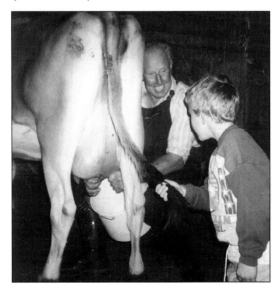

My son Harry in 1953, demonstrating the way milking was done! (C. Pursey)

My dad hand-milking a Jersey cow, which he did twice daily until 1997 when ill health forced him to retire. My son, Kevin, is gently restraining the cow's tail to stop her from flicking it into his grandfather's face. Kevin was fascinated by the procedure, despite the fact that his own dad milks 165 cows twice daily in a modern milking parlour. I reckon he's a lucky wee boy to have witnessed a dying tradition. (Sandra Beggs)

My grandfather, James Charles Turner, third from the right, known as Charl, learned his craft at the knee of his father, James Turner, in the narrow confines of Five Ways, Birmingham, in the latter part of the last century. James Turner migrated to the city from rural Derbyshire about the middle of the nineteenth century; his father, William Turner, born in the last year of the eighteenth century, was a small farmer and basket maker in Oakthorpe. When Charles finished his life's craft in the late 1970s, in Birch Road, Oldbury, so ended a line of rural craftsmen of at least four generations. (Peter Charles Turner)

Cutting the corn in the late 1930s. In the small mixed farms in Ulster in the '30s and '40s, most of the work was manual with the help of horse-drawn machines. It was a family affair with neighbours helping. The photo shows a brother (sitting) and sister and a friend with a horse reaper which cut the corn (oats). It was then tied by hand into sheaves and put into stooks (three or four sheaves) put together vertically. (William McKeown)

This image is one of a series taken from an ongoing personal photographic project recording the historic and traditional activity of harvesting rush at Isle Abbot on the Somerset levels. The rubber dinghy is not in itself an attractive element but it does bring the image into the late twentieth century. In contrast, the female workers could be placed at any time between the '60s and '90s. The inclusion of the children shows this to be a family event and demonstrates parental responsibility, in that the boat is attached to the parent by a cord which is tied around her waist as she works. (Caroline Bagias)

This is me, Valerie Hicks, outside the butcher's shop my husband and I ran in 1984. It was situated in Walkley in Sheffield. This was then a very busy shopping area; there were lots of small shops like ours, creating a wonderfully caring community. But tastes change and progress moves on and unfortunately our little family butcher's along with many more are lost. They are now a thing of the past and our grandchildren will never know the skill it took to be what my husband was so proud to be – a master butcher. (Mrs V.C. Hicks)

This photo was taken at a factory office in Chorley, Lancashire, in about 1963. The start of the computer age! I am in the far corner, near the door. The girls used to punch information from invoices etc. on to small cards, with the smaller of the two machines you can see, passed it to another girl to verify, and if correct she would double punch it. We were paid a flat rate and as you got faster you were paid a proficiency bonus of 7s 6d a week! The cards were then sent to the computer which in those days took a full room. Things have come a long way since those early days! (Margaret Milner)

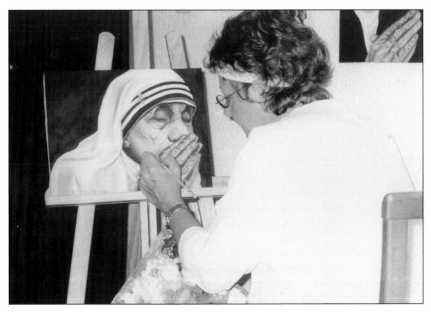

When I first saw this lady's face, the deep sunken eyes, the wrinkles, the worn, weathered hands from years of dedication to the poor and dying, I saw the selflessness and strength – the ultimate faith in God. I was so inspired that I knew, as an artist, I had to get this fabulous face on canvas. During my fourth painting, she died. I was overwhelmed to hear that the Pope was to canonise her during the Millennium. As the world is today with all its horrors, one can truly know for sure that this wonderful lady's goodness will be a magnificent inspiration to our future generations. (Adele Van der Velde)

Taken in February 1994, this shows Dave Heath (Hoskyns) with Dave Grayland of Brintons in the computer room. Outsourcing was seen by many companies at the time as a way of reducing high labour costs at a time of recessions, by removing in-house computer staff including me, allowing the few left to concentrate on implementing new, client-server based packages. From the staff, already culled by redundancies, some twelve people became Hoskyns staff and travelled to Birmingham daily to support the systems. (Joan Margaret Page)

Susan Macpherson, my daughter, aged 2, feeding the milkman's horse in June 1956 at Durrington on Sea, Worthing, West Sussex: a pleasure widely available then, especially for children. The horse-drawn float has disappeared and the milkman is an endangered species. (A. Macpherson)

This is a photograph of my father, Thomas John Davies, taken in the Caerphilly Town area in around 1955. He was then a refuse lorry driver with Caerphilly UDC in the days when drivers did nothing but drive. I believe the vehicle was a Dennis and had a peculiar steering mechanism, no steering wheel but left and right handles, and the driver sat in the middle of the cab. It was ideal for the narrow lanes behind terraced houses that at the time abounded in the town. Note the castle leaning tower which was CUDC's emblem. (Anne Phillips)

I took this photo of my grandad, Angus John Monk, making hay in the laughter-filled late summer day in 1994. My mum and dad are in the background and even though not visible, my granny and my sister Ciorstaidh were helping too. Historically, I feel this photograph is important as it shows a family working together using a technology that has been in use for generations still being used in late twentieth-century Britain. In the future, this method may only be seen in photographs as, here in the Outer Hebrides, new, less people-intensive technologies are taking over. (Sorcha Monk)

I took this photo on 6 June 1956, about a hundred yards from my home at Tredegar, South Wales. There were no pit-head baths at Ty Trist colliery so the miners are walking home in their working clothes, their faces black with coal dust. Ty Trist was opened in 1834 and closed in 1959, and it was the colliery where many of the latest inventions in mining were tried out. A leisure centre stands on the site today and a road now runs in place of the railway line, but many buildings of the mill farm are still standing. (Gordon Hayward)

This is a photo of my work at ICI in Billingham, Cleveland, where I was a chemical processing engineer on the ammonia plants. Billingham was the largest producer of ammonia, producing about 4,000 tons every twenty-four hours, with a usage of 10% natural gas in the UK; it also had the biggest compressor in the world. Plants 1,2 and 3 have shut down and are currently being demolished; only plant 4 survives. Russia began exporting cheap ammonia to Europe undercutting all producers: this began the decline of ICI as an ammonia producer. After shutdown in 1991, today again there is a shortage of ammonia. (Eric Wright)

This photograph, taken in 1910 in Sheepscar, Leeds, is of my mother, Eleanor Targus, née Leslie, and her mother Lilian Leslie, the owner of the shop. Note the newspaper billboards recording the events of the day and the extensive advertising in the shop windows. (Marjorie Targus)

George Webb was a well-known cobbler in Newtown for over 50 years. Apprenticed at the Hospital for Poor Souls before joining the Army (1914–18), he opened his shop in the early '20s. To add to his income he took in wireless batteries for collection to be charged. I remember a box of valves and wires from which, as a hobby, he made a wireless and the excitement when he turned a dial and music could be heard – it was magic. In the Second World War business improved because of rationing as shoes were repaired more. This enabled him to buy an electric motor for his finishing machine to replace the manual treadle. (J. Leavesley)

The picture shows miners from Yorkshire protesting outside the Houses of Parliament in spring 1992. These were the final death throes of the British mining industry. It was a time when mining communities throughout the country finally lost their fight to keep deep mining pits open; it was also a time when trade unions were significantly reduced in size and power. It was a turning point for some, as computers became more important, but some areas in the north never recovered. (John Wilkinson)

This is my friend, one of a special breed of men who go out to sea each day to bring us fish in all weathers. He owns his small trawler after years of struggle to make it pay. He says with a laugh that it has to be a vocation because nobody would work the long hours for the money. Week after week, bombarded with new regulations from Brussels, fish quotas, mesh sizes, more paperwork, the list goes on. It is a way of life ebbing away like the tide. (Norman Pascoe)

This is my grandfather, Stanley Reed, outside his shoe repair shop on Westbourne Avenue, Bensham, Gateshead, in the early 1930s. He ran the cobbler shop for over forty years and lived in the house attached to the shop where my mother still lives today. Everything in the shop went to Beamish Museum, where hopefully it is to be rebuilt. Note the old gas lamp on the left, and my grandfather's motorbike on the right. The house once belonged to a Judge – the Rt Hon Walter Henry Baron Northbourne – until September 1900. (Hazel Allen)

While working on replacing an old gas main with a new plastic one, we had to work nights. The work was alongside the train lines, and at one stage a policeman had come to where we were working as an old lady thought aliens had landed as she could see strange lights. After four nights' solid work, we completed the project. (Steven Hillman)

Pam King, magicienne and puppeteer. At the time that this photograph was taken in May 1997, Pam King was a fully qualified member of the magic circle. The magic circle had 1400 male members and just twenty-five female members. Pam King was the second female to be admitted to this exclusive organisation. The first was Debbie McGee, wife of TV personality Paul Daniels. One of the things Pam liked doing most was appearing at children's shows with 'Punch and Judy'. Sadly, Pam died in 1998. How much longer will Punch and Judy last? (Lindsay Heywood)

This machine is a fine example of British engineering and a tribute to the people who carried out the restoration. Built in 1927 by Robeys of Lincoln, it was rescued from a scrapyard by a Mr Rundle and then bought in 1959 by its present owner Richard Booty, who is responsible for the restoration. The photograph shows it being driven to a site to raise money for charity. I hope there will be dedicated people in the twenty-first century who will learn the skills of our ancestors and help to continue our heritage. (R.D. Myers)

This is a photograph of my father, Charles Richard Haynes, aged 20, gathering in the hay on his father's farm in Old Marston, Oxford, in 1933. In those days, every aspect of farming was labour intensive. Even in his short lifetime he saw massive leaps in farming technology that sounded the death knoll for farm workers world-wide. This photograph reminds me how hard life was then and not some long lost halcyon days that are forever gone. Yet he dearly loved his way of life. (Rosemarie Martin)

This is a photograph taken of factory girls leaving after a day's work at the 'Worlsback', near Wandsworth High Street/West Hill in south-west London in the early 1920s. In the centre of the group of five is my mother, May Macey then aged about 18. After leaving school at 14 she found that live-in domestic service was not to her liking. The pay was five shillings per week, seven days a week with one afternoon off. She found she could make ten times that amount hand stitching gas mantles which were still used to light most London schools up until 1950. (Peter Macey)

A photo of my dad (Arthur Day) taken in 1987, the year he retired after more than forty years 'on the buses'. The bus shown is route 11 and was one of his main routes covering the most popular tourist attractions – and as a Londoner I hope the red double-decker bus will remain as part of our heritage. (Ellen Wilson)

My brother-in-law Henry Philip Davies at Barry Island Bus Park, 1950. Barry was the day excursion destination for Valley families. At this time he was 25 and had just changed jobs from the other Caerphilly Bus Company, the Greys. As employment was easy to come by in the aftermath of the war Henry regularly swapped jobs from one company to the other. (J.B. Phillips)

My grandfather outside his saddlery in Stirling Road, Glasgow, in the company of his apprentices, 1920s. Unfortunately for his descendants, he'd sunk the family fortunes into a business that was doomed to failure for it was just at this period of the twentieth century that horses were disappearing as a means of transport. Now if only he had invested in a garage.... (Alistair Stirling)

This is a photo of Fred Oliver Smith, known locally as the Bull. He was head gamekeeper on the Lord Daresbury Estates, Higher Walton, Warrington, Lancashire, and the place he lived was known as the kennels. The photograph was taken in approximately 1924 and he is seen here holding four fox cubs which were cared for by his daughter Dolly. Whenever possible after the hunts she would rescue and tame these orphans and keep them as pets with her father. It seems he was very fond of the cunning fox. Fred died in 1944, aged 80 years. (Mrs L.E. Smith)

PC Malcolm Pugh posing at a Newton Aycliffe training session, in March 1999. On several occasions over the last twenty-one years, I have had to don this type of equipment: a necessary requirement in the twentieth century. I performed duty at the Toxteth riots. Later, during the miners' strike, I was part of a convoy of police vehicles on the motorway. The convoy stretched as far as the eye could see, both to the front and to the rear. I was part of history in the making. It will never be seen again. Hard times indeed. (Malcolm Pugh)

Most County Durham villages had their own coal mine at some point in the last hundred years, providing employment on the doorstep – no need to travel to work. The photograph shows the Hawthorn Combined Mine situated between the villages of South Hetton and Murton, both of which also had their own colliery systems. Hawthorn was a large modern inland plant, complete with its own coke works, but here in 1974 it provides the backdrop for a machine of the past, the industrial steam engine. Coal mining is now only a memory in Durham, with the last colliery closing during the 1980s. (Ray Kitching)

play

I was a photographer on the Brighton and Hove seafront for about forty years, mostly on the Palace Pier. This photo, for me, typified the day-trippers. It was taken in front of the Palace Pier Gates in the 1950s. I think it caught the joy and 'out for the day' pleasure. (Ron Stuart, **Winner**)

My grandad taking third place in a Knobbly Knees competition at Butlins holiday camp in 1962. Masses of people flocked to those camps that were all situated around the coast of the UK. You can see the spectators in the background all huddled up against the wind and in the distance the cable car which was a standard feature of these camps. Each morning the holidaymakers were greeted over a large speaker with 'Morning campers' and announcements were made throughout the day directing people around the camp. The '60s were the real heyday of British holiday camps. (Katharine Krysula Wright, Pontefract New College, **Secondary School Winner**)

My Nana's two friends on a church trip walking in the French Alps sometime in the 1920s. The photo is of personal value because it is of two of my Nana's closest friends on one of their favourite trips. The photo is of historic value and will be of interest to future generations because of the clothes they are wearing. The footwear is totally unsuitable – the women have heels on their shoes and they are walking in the Alps! The weather would be freezing, yet they have skirts on; and their coats wouldn't have been warm. You can tell they are high up as they are roped together for safety! One of them could easily have broken an ankle with walking in those shoes. I think you will agree this picture is very interesting! (Rachel Nicholson, St Wilfrid's CE High School, **Secondary School Winner**)

This photograph was taken in August 1936. It shows my mother, then aged 19, with a group of Guide Rangers on a cycling holiday to Germany. My mother, then called Lily Henshall, is on the far left of the group, which is posed ready to set off from the Hotel Schweizer-Hof in Cologne. Holidays abroad were quite unusual in those days – especially by a group of young women. During the holiday my mother and her friends were impressed by the politeness of the young men they met who were invariably in uniform and very gallant. The friends did not realise at the time that they were witnessing the military build-up to the Second World War. (Anita Varey, **Winner**)

Five younger members of my family. I am the young player on the right, playing my brother on the left, who is two years older. The photograph was taken by my oldest brother, who was eighteen years older than me. Although we never had many luxuries of life, I experienced a very happy childhood. (James Sammons, **Winner**)

Me and my younger brother on 2 June 1953, the day of the Coronation of Queen Elizabeth II, on Tedstone Road, Harborne, Birmingham. We held a street party to celebrate and everyone decorated their houses with flags. On the 'green' playground they brought out their tables and chairs and held a children's tea party. Afterwards, the children dressed up for a fancy-dress competition, followed by sports races in the road. Some of us children were very lucky to watch the Coronation on a small picture screen that was new and called 'television'. (G.J. Gascoyne)

Me on the right of the picture and my brother Ron on the left, then aged 6 and 5 respectively. The photograph was snapped by our Uncle George in the garden of our grandparents at Acton, London, in 1932. For a pictorial time record I believe this photo captures the sheer innocence of those past, distant days when a simple bunch of keys could hold fascination to children who today would look for 'Star Wars' games on a computer screen! (Cyril Kellman, **Runner Up**)

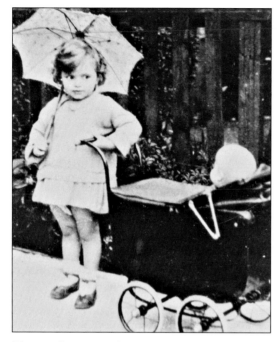

This is a photograph of my wife, Dorothy Christian, aged 3, when she lived in Salford in 1932. This was the time when little girls were happy to play with dolls and childhood was the happiest time of their lives. Imagination played a very big part in children's minds those days, and you can see that without all the advantages that modern children have, life was just as much fun. (C.A. Christian)

Me and a friend as children, at Esh in Durham, during the storms of 1963. The snow was so deep that we were able to sit on top of a signpost. Because of recent climate changes, we don't get such heavy snow falls any more, and may never do so again. (Shirley Sharp, **Runner Up**)

My uncles Harry and George Sammons in Worcester Park, London, 1936, preparing to set off for a 90-mile round trip to Brighton, a ride they regularly made until they were called up for the Second World War. Both returned safely to enjoy the pleasures of cycling again. Increased use of motor cars have led to fewer people cycling, but my family still enjoys it. Green transport plans mean that cycling may once again become a popular form of transport. (Marion Pusey, **Runner Up**)

Me and friend Don Ward practising our acrobatic act at the Stewponey Lido near Stourbridge, 1960. The entrance fee of 2s enabled you to stay all day, and some families with modest means would spend their holidays at the lido, commuting daily by bus which was part of a well-integrated service in those days. Many reasons hastened the demise of lidos, not least the British weather. This shows what some people did in their leisure time in a less frenetic age. (Bob Broadfield, **The *Express* Runner Up**)

A little girl, rising 9, reads a bedtime story to her 4-year-old brother, from James Roose-Evans' *The Adventures of Odd and Elsewhere*. He is spellbound, his imagination at once captured by his sister's story telling and the idea that the story can come from a book. The girl would go on to become a teacher of English at Castleford High School, Wakefield, and the boy to read Law at Leeds University. Both living in Leeds, they still enjoy the easy companionship so evident in this photograph of May 1983. They are my children, Catharine (born 1974) and David (born 1979) in David's bedroom at 18 Kelsey Crescent, Cherryhinton, Cambridge. (Bruce Purvis, **Runner-Up**)

My nana is in the photo of a street party to celebrate the silver wedding anniversary of George V and Queen Mary in 1936. In the background, you can see a miner, just returned from his shift. In those days, they didn't have pit baths and miners had to come home black from all the coal dust. (Wendy Gowen, **Runner-Up**)

This photo was taken in Avenue Road, Great Malvern, on Saturday 25 March 1950. At that time, colleges were becoming more available to youngsters and the way they 'let off steam' after studying was to have a Rag Week, culminating in a Rag Day. Their ingenuity knew no bounds. Chamber pots were affixed to steeples, midnight picnics enjoyed and Rag Day itself had a carnival procession, many local traders lending lorries to be decorated to a theme. This photo shows the reconstruction of the Malvern Girls' College, 'manned' by girls in the school uniform, a despised mistress hanging from gallows, the school nurse administering medicine to the 'girls', all pupils at the College of Electronics, Malvern, and largely members of the rugby team. (Mrs M. Tompkins, **Runner-Up**)

This is a photograph of my 3-year-old son Joshua, taken last summer, entering the playing fields of the village of Whitmore in Staffordshire. In a world where over-protective parents live in fear that their child may become the victim of some perverse crime, abduction or even the unimaginable – death, this photograph encapsulates the 'lost innocence of youth', which may never, sadly, be recaptured again. (Mr Franco Scibetta, **Runner-Up**)

My brother Paul in the early 1970s. Then, we were oblivious to the 'trouble' going on around us. Our father put our swing on the lamppost for us and we spent many carefree hours swinging and fighting over whose turn it was. The road along the top of the picture was Ormeau Avenue; it divided us from the Protestant community. The concrete blocks or Dragon's Teeth behind my brother were put there to stop a recurrence of a car bomb being pushed down the street, but to us they were just something to be swung on. (Susan Watson, **Runner-Up**)

This picture was taken in 1978. I remember the lion tamer's name was Hans Dieter Muck. Animal circus acts are much less popular now than they were in the earlier part of this century, when the world was still being explored and the bravery of the lion tamer and his mastery over the king of the animal kingdom was admired and held in awe. Now the earth seems a more fragile place, with wild animals threatened everywhere by the destruction of their environment. The lion tamer's bravery is less admired and the better the animals perform, the more would be the suspicion that cruelty had been employed in training them. The lion pacing the length of its small cage repeatedly is not aggressive, but mentally ill through the torture of confinement. (John Storr, **Runner-Up**)

This picture was taken on 24 April 1999, at the time of the Kosovan War. I have chosen this to show how, although my country is at war, it has not affected life in England: my life is not changed at all. However, for those in Kosovo and surrounding areas, life is changed, and often ruined. This picture also shows one of the most important things in my life, friendship. I think this is of historic importance as it shows future generations the feelings of an ordinary teenager in the twentieth century – friendship is everything. (Sarah Tuley, Ashford School)

This is a photograph of me on a school trip to London. I'm the child in the cream coat. Apart from this picture being a good group shot, the Yeoman of the Guard or 'Beefeater' represents something very British. The Yeomen of the Guard have guarded the Tower of London throughout its history as it changed from a prison to a fortress, a royal residence and recently a museum, always wearing their traditional Tudor uniform. What I also like about this photograph are the children's hairstyles and clothes – both of which set this photograph in the early 1970s. (Miss L. Walker)

My neighbour's children playing in the back courts of the old Govan tenements in Glasgow in 1966 (long since demolished). Thankfully, today's children will not experience the slum conditions of these years. This photograph reminds us that many children still play in conditions such as this in many underdeveloped countries around the world. (Philip Gruner)

My uncle preparing a barbecue at a family get-together. He is in charge of the barbecue as lots of men are on sunny days in England. (Camilla Addison)

This is my first ever trip to London, 1966. Stuff the Palace and all the museums, I wanted to experience the excitement of the newest, tallest building – after all it was the 'swinging sixties'. My sister and her boyfriend had to endure the ear popping trip up the Post Office Tower and then pay for twenty minutes in the revolving restaurant. My own children think it's sad to wear a school blazer during a Saturday day out but the uniform was the only smart outfit I had! (Mr N.J. Cronin)

Girl Guides from the East End of London, camping in Folkestone in the 1920s. My mother is the guide captain (with rather too fashionable shoes!) on the extreme right, with three marvellous Girl Guide types and the laundry in the background. This photo reflects the historic 'guiding' tradition of the East End; and apart from Hopping, this will have been the only sort of holiday that young women will have had. My mother never stopped talking about how wonderful her guiding days were and I was press-ganged at the end of the 1940s into joining my local Girl Guides. I just couldn't get out of it! (Janet Capon Neri)

The photograph was taken in the mid-'50s. It shows me (left), my wife Barbara Julia (centre) and my wife's twin sister Margaret on the right. At the time petrol was rationed owing to the Suez crisis. We saved the coupons for enough petrol to go on a camping trip in our 1935 Morris 8 two-door saloon in the background. (Harry Edwards)

The Lambeg Drum playing in the field in an Orange demonstration in the 1940s. The men in front played fifes, but could hardly be heard above the din of the massive drums. At this period, these drums were very popular with rural Orange Lodges and some families were noted drummers. Drumming contests were common in the summer time. (William McKeown)

This shows three fellows taking a rest on a bike outing to Slemish Mountain in April 1962. Slemish was where St Patrick was supposed to have herded pigs. Cars were a luxury in the early 1960s and few young men had one, so cycles were a favourite form of transport. (William McKeown)

This is a photo of my father, Leo, (seated on the grass to the right of the picture) taken in 1952 with his mixed sex and ethnic hockey team whilst studying for a degree in Agriculture at Borough Polytechnic, now named Southbank University. I think it captures a unique period of British post-war history and shows how the sons and daughters of the British empire had a presence in this country before and just after the Second World War, either studying in the armed services, or as professionals. (Guy Regis)

Above: I took this photo when I was at school in Newcastle upon Tyne in 1983. The boys were not known to me but struck this spontaneous pose when they saw the camera. This look was entirely natural at the time and will evoke memories for anybody who was a teenager in the '70s or early '80s. Some parents wrote to complain about the picture bringing the school into disrepute: exactly the kind of reaction teenagers of any generation try to provoke. (Nicholas Posner)

Left: I took this picture in August 1998 at Gloucester Docks on a club outing. I called it 'sheer fascination' – the colour and the clothes epitomised the times. The trainers, the clown's shades, cap and jacket: the picture has what I feel a good picture should have – a sense of mystery. Exactly what is the clown doing? Will we ever know? It does not matter to us, but to the little children undoubtedly it will be a day they will never forget. (Brian Barnett)

My husband Samuel on our first holiday as boyfriend and girlfriend. We went with my parents. He is pretending to be Samson at the great stones of Stonehenge. It was taken in the very early 1970s and all visitors were free to mill around, touch and sit on the stones. It reflects the relaxed, carefree attitude there was in visiting our heritage sites before the thought of preservation for future generations, before the fear of vandalism, before the revival of paganism. No one was in any way paying homage to or revering the stones. We were all simply well-behaved tourists. (Mrs Linda Paxton)

The British Olympic cycle track and Olympic road racing team and officials. This was at a reception given by Dunlop Rubber Co. at Fort Dunlop. I was in charge of organising training and selection of the road team. Owing to the number of crashes on Richmond Park circuit, only one British rider finished. In the centre front is Reg Harris who went on to become Pro Sprint Champion of the World until he retired. This was the first Olympics after the Second World War. (Mr Arthur Robert Millett)

The picture, taken in 1922, shows my father in the front row on the right. It was a local team consisting of miners in Yorkshire. They played hard and worked hard. The ships, trains and homes all used local coal. He started work at 12 and retired at 65. He was a gentleman and wore his best suit at weekends with a bowler hat and well-polished shoes. Wartime made miners very important and they got extra rations. (Mrs Margaret Sims)

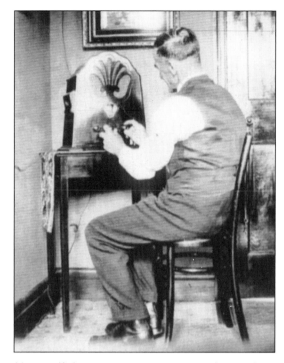

My grandfather concentrating on tuning his wireless, 1930s. My mother won a prize in a local newspaper for this photograph. The wireless is long gone, but I still have the picture which is of flamingos painted on glass, also the chair on which my grandfather is sitting. How simple and unsophisticated that wireless seems compared to what is available today, but my grandfather was quite content with it for his entertainment. (Dorothy Rand)

My mother Hilda Davies is the one wearing white; she is on a day out with friends in Yorkshire, 1930. There always seemed to be something going on in the community. People helped each other. I remember going to the local cinema matinée with her to see Gracie Fields. Holidays took place in August in Blackpool. We used to book for cooking and attention, which meant we bought the food and the landlady cooked it. (Margaret Sims)

My husband, Kenneth Hall, and his twin brother, Gary, on a day trip to South Shields. That's when a trip to the beach meant exactly that. You didn't need £40 in your pocket to keep the kids amused as you do today; they were content with sand, sea, a few sandwiches, a drink of pop and their imagination, a recipe for a perfect day. (Mrs C. Hall)

This is me aged 7 in the garden on a winter's morning. It had snowed the night before, but in the morning the sun came out and it melted, so I gathered as much as I could to make two snowmen. I remember being so proud. I am now 15. My mum said when she was young the snow would last a week and not just a day. (Stephanie Cowie)

Three friends out on a Sunday walk in 1946. We went for long walks in those days (we could not afford cars like present day teenagers). Posing beside a council steamroller, we were wrapped up for the weekend. You can also see a haystack in the background. (Ronald Pears)

My mother (left, wearing glasses) with neighbours in 1952 at the back court of the tenement buildings in Dundas Street, Grangemouth, Stirlingshire, where we lived. They were taking a well-earned break from washing clothes in the wash-house by having a game of skipping. My sister Sarah is the little girl running towards them. We children enjoyed this break from the mother's routine as much as they did. This photo reflects an era when money was not in great abundance but happiness and community spirit were. (Rose Donaldson)

This is a photo of a couple we met on holiday on the Isle of Man in 1956. I had a motorcycle and they hired a scooter and we toured all over the island. No helmets or protective gear in those days. (Ronald Pears)

My dad when he was 2 years old. He was on holiday at Skegness in 1962. The dog belonged to the photographer who worked for the 'Linga Longa Photo Shop', Skegness. I think my dad looks cute, wearing his cardigan with soldiers on it. (Kirsty Allen)

Flower power was all the rage when this photo was taken in the late '60s. We were staying at a hotel in Sandown, Isle of Wight at the time that John and Yoko were staging their bed sit-in. So we went to the fancy dress parade as them and won first prize. We were such a good look-a-like that when we walked along the prom we were almost mobbed – what fun British holidays were! (Mr and Mrs J. Parker)

Me at my primary school May fair with my head teacher, dressed as Robin Hood. I can remember being shy and quiet but the day was full of excitement. This demonstrates the tradition of having a May Queen every year but the event is dying out slowly, as has the tradition of maypole dancing. (Stephanie Cowie)

Me and my friend Kate at a '70s night in Planet Earth nightclub, Leeds, 1997. We also worked there and got dressed up in our wigs and flares every Saturday to work behind the bar! This picture captures a trend in the nightclub scene of the '90s – to go back to the '70s, and boogie on down! (Paula Garwood)

This was taken in 1915 at an open-air café on the Malvern Hills. My parents, not yet married, are taking a raspberry and cream tea. Father is wearing his South African War ribbons (including a DCM) and is flashing his brand new RSM rank badges. Taking the photo was my Aunt Jessie. (Colin Reid)

Jean Desforges (aged 7) wins a race during the street party in Stork Road, Forest Gate, London E7, as part of the celebrations for the Coronation of George VI in 1937. Jean went on to compete in the 1952 Olympic Games in Helsinki – fifth in the 80 m Hurdles, Bronze medal in the 4 × 100 m relay and became European Long Jump Champion in 1954. When son Shaun Desforges Pickering (aged 34) competed in the shotput event at Atlanta in 1996, they became the first mother and son Olympians to compete in track and field for Great Britain. (Jean Pickering)

This photo was taken by my father, A.H. Sleigh, in February 1960 when Billy Smart's Circus visited King's Lynn. The elephant is clearly enjoying himself, the member of the audience might be and the rest probably did. Travelling circuses with performing animals will probably be confined to the history books in the next century, but will the animals mind? (John Sleigh)

This photograph is of personal value to me because it shows me and my sister with Mickey Mouse in EuroDisney where I always wanted to go. We are getting his autograph. It will be of historic value because Mickey Mouse is the most famous cartoon character of the twentieth century. People from all over the world like to visit him in America and France. Who knows? Perhaps he will still be around in 100 years' time. (Ashleigh Plunkett, St Clare's School, **Primary School Winner**)

Above: We think this is School Sports Day in 1928 at Huntingdon Grammar School and we know it was the girls' 100 yards race. You can see by their faces they are very serious but I think their sports gear is very unhygienic and would slow them down a lot. Compare it with modern sports gear which is mainly Lycra and streamlined. Can you see what has not changed?, Look at the umbrellas! (Claire Ward, St Teresa's RC Primary School, **Primary School Winner**)

Left: My dad in 1988. It is special to my dad because it was when he was able 'to get away from it all'. He was in Wales because he wanted to have a break from work. In the picture he is on a hill looking at the sea. He was 23 when this photo was taken. He had a rucksack on his back that had food and drink in it because he needed it to live. He had a lot more climbing to do until he got to the top. He was very tired when he got there. He still likes the countryside and now we often walk together. (Alexandra Harvey, St Mary's RC School, **Primary School Winner**)

This was taken from the album of my great-aunt by marriage, Emmeline Beck née Langford. She trained as a nurse in Exeter at the turn of the century and when the old hospital was still in use I remember seeing her name as a silver medallist on the awards board in the Nursing School. This photo shows the nurses from a hospital ship moored off Alexandria in 1916 being taken sightseeing to Sakkara near Cairo. This was as near as nurses were allowed to the front line at that time. (Dr Jane Richards)

My cousin and I went for a run for our ice creams, 1952. At that time, there were no amusement arcades and the whole pleasure of our innocent lives was to be beside the sea. I think this photograph captures the British seaside as it used to be. (Daniel Leigh Gregory)

This is a photo of my dad and my brother Peter in 1962 on the Sussex farm where we lived. My dad is holding up a large cod that he caught on a rod and line from the beach at Pevensey, on one of his Friday night fishing trips. Severe depletion of fish stocks means it is now almost impossible to catch anything from the beach and sadly my dad no longer fishes. The farm where the photo was taken was compulsorily purchased in the 1970s to make way for an access road to an out-of-town shopping centre. (Sue M. Walton)

I have selected this Prestatyn beach photograph, taken in July 1926, as it depicts a typical lower middle-class family on holiday. No special beach outfits, the straw hats would be part of the traditional wardrobe at home in Liverpool. Only the upper middle class and rich could afford those, though canvas shoes were usually worn on the beach to protect the leather from the salt. Although deckchairs have been hired, perhaps the weather was uncertain for a longer stay. My outfit is beautifully crocheted in artificial silk yarn, the vogue, by my aunt or grandmother. (Mrs I.A. Sanders)

The historical interest in this photograph is the vehicle – a solid-tyred truck of the 1920s. I do not know the make for certain, but it could be a Dennis. The photo depicts an incident in the Cardiff University Rag Week of 1928/9. I am seated in the middle of the lower part of the truck. (Mrs M. Thompson)

This is a photo of my dad and grandad at the Festival of Britain in 1951. My dad was 7 years old and my grandad was 40 years old. They are standing by an original Henry Moore sculpture which was made especially for the Festival. I think that this is an important part of history because the Festival of Britain celebrated Britain's achievements and conquests. The whole reason for the Festival of Britain was to boost people's morale after five hard years of war and many more years of rations and limited supplies. (Alex Gibson, Kesteven & Grantham Girls' School)

This is a photograph of me when I was 5 in 1955. I am leading the procession in the white cardigan, knitted for me by my grandma. I am taking part in the May Day celebrations in Brentham in the London Borough of Ealing. Traditionally, every year a May Queen was chosen and after a procession with her attendants through the streets, there was folk dancing, including the Maypole Dance. The girls wore white dresses with spring flowers in their hair and carried posies of flowers and ribbons on sticks. (Pamela Crisp)

My state school, Hearnville Road, Balham, celebrating Empire Day after the war in the late 1940s. All the flag carrying children had to wear Cub or Brownie uniforms or national costumes. The pupils chosen to do the dancing display wore white – even the boys. Parents were proud to kit out their children. We enjoyed the celebration. It helped us to learn about the Empire and what it meant to England. (Dame Shirley Oxenbury)

This is a photo of the King's Messengers; the date is 1 July 1911. Somewhere on it is my Uncle Bill. I have really no other information. Even so, it is a part of my village's history and a copy of this photo is going to the Eastham Historical Society. (Mrs R.F. Abraham)

Left: A street party for Queen Elizabeth's Coronation, in Notting Hill Gate, 1953. The lady standing on the left of the photograph is my great-grandmother, Margo Buckingham. Directly in front of her, the boy in the suit looking towards the camera is my grandfather's brother, Norman and the boy opposite him is my grandfather, David. I feel that it would be relevant to future generations because we do not seem to have street parties any more. I am 9 years old and have never been to a street party. Also, my grandfather at the time of the picture is 12 years old. It seems strange to think that he was once nearly as young as me. Finally, it gives a real sense of community and not many people have photos of their great-grandmother. (Emma Buckingham)

Right: We were on a week's holiday at Voryn Hall holiday camp in Old Colwyn. My mother, father and aunt came on a day trip from Liverpool to visit us. I am amazed at the change of style of leisurewear in forty years! My father dressed in his 'best' three-piece suit, complete with hat and pocket watch. My mother was also wearing a full-length coat and hat. Similarly my mother-in-law wore a full-length coat and hat on a coach trip to Middleton Towers, Morecambe. (Mrs M. Wilkinson)

Left: A picture of my grandfather on holiday in Weymouth in 1938. He is 8 years old in the photograph. This picture shows me that people went on holiday to the seaside even in the 1930s. Such holidays must have been popular as you can see hotels in the background. The name of the hotel – The Victoria – also suggests that holidays at the seaside went back to the beginning of the century and Queen Victoria's reign. I think that it is interesting that my grandfather is riding a donkey as this is still a common beach entertainment today. (Joseph Plant)

Providing the muscle in a bit of horseplay with his brother-in-law on a beach in his parents' native Northern Ireland. This is my great-grandfather C.R. Magill, in June 1938, enjoying the simple pleasures of that uncomplicated generation. Within a few short months, millions of people's lives were changed. On a personal note, within two years of this photograph being taken, my grandmother's father, a private in the Lancashire Fusiliers, lost his life, also on a beach, the victim of a land mine in the British retreat at Dunkirk. (Lucy Futcher)

By the time these two little girls reach their 70th or maybe even their 17th birthdays, they will have forgotten all about their contribution to Red Nose Day on 12 March 1999. Yet it was a day millions of people throughout Britain wore bright red in aid of charity. These two little friends on the school field are just a tiny but important part of a huge network in motion to provide much-needed funds for the unfortunates of this world. Will these wonderful days continue? I fear not, but who knows? (Mrs Joan Maddra)

My late husband's friends in the mid-1930s before hostilities had been even thought of. Charabancs were opening up the way for a trip or weekend at the seaside, especially to Margate, Kent, from the London area. They certainly made the most of life, as you can see, with sing-alongs, providing laughter for the rest of the year with their antics. (Valerie Brooke)

My uncle and his friend in around 1940. I think this was a spoof on the famous *Picture Post* cover of two women on the seafront. They were part of a group who toured all over the country by bike. Their idea of a perfect weekend was travelling to a different place – fresh air, good food, good company and plenty of exercise. Soon after this photo was taken, my uncle was called up and spent three and a half years as a Japanese prisoner of war. When he came home, he said he would never leave this country again, and he never did. (Sylvia Conway)

This is a picture of Derek (left) and me in Linwood, Scotland, in the summer of 1967. It is memorable to me as it was a time when friends played on their doorstep – no need for computers or designer trainers. These were new council houses in the 1960s occupied by young families for the first time. They mainly came from Glasgow to work in a boom town, because of the wealth of jobs in the car industry, pressed steel, etc. (Frank Emonds)

At the end of the twentieth century there are many more pensioners and they are leading a full and active life, even if they have to seek assistance to get about by using scooters, stair lifts, etc. This is a picture of John and Geraldine Mitchell in the Oxfordshire countryside in 1996, taken by John's son Michael. (Geraldine Mitchell)

If pictures are to be believed, it would appear that in the early 1960s fishing, albeit only for tiddlers, was just as popular with the girls as with the boys. (Mr E.C. Smith)

This is a photo taken by me aged 10 in 1957, showing a typical family seaside trip. The venue was Hayling Island, Hants. The Austin Cambridge was my father's car, the Ford Anglia belonged to my Uncle Dennis and the Hillman FB Minx belonged to my Uncle Maurice who is standing in front of the Hillman. In those days, it used to be fun to rendezvous with the family and a trip to the seaside was an adventure. Driving was easy with usually plenty of places to park. Today, a trip to the coast in the summer is a nightmare! (Clive Howard Litten)

Hood Fayre near Totnes in Devon was one of the many alternative summer entertainments to spring up in the mid-'80s. Hippie culture met fringe art and alternative chic. I was amused from where I was standing at the band's apparent lack of audience. (Roy Perring)

My name is Welbeck. I shall never forget the day I went to the FA Cup semi-final between Liverpool and Nottingham Forest, 15 April 1989, at Hillsborough. I made a splendid figure, 17 hands high, superbly trained for my job as a police horse. Play was abandoned after six minutes as millions watched on television the worst disaster in the history of British football. As crowds were crushed against the barriers, ninety-five people died. I was knocked down, trampled and traumatised. I found my healing in Redwings Horse Sanctuary in Norfolk. (Mrs B. Sheila Redclift)

The photograph shows a family day out at the Edinburgh Festival Cavalcade. This procession heralds the start of the world famous Arts Festival, held annually since 1947. The 2CV Car Club of Great Britain took part in 1998 to celebrate the 2CV's fiftieth birthday. Britain has hundreds of car clubs whose members have great affection for their classic cars. The leading car belongs to Joe and Zara Cent, founder club members in Scotland. I also had a car in the procession. My first 2CV was bought in 1975 during the world oil crisis. (Robert W. Cunningham)

'The Rocky Horror Picture Show'. I took this photograph at the 'warm-up' prior to the show at the Guildhall, Portsmouth. This musical has become a cult show of modern times with over half the audience dressing (or undressing) for each performance. In this particular performance they used on-stage pyrotechnics which nearly blew me up as I photographed from the wings. (Richard Cooke)

As a child, I loved going to the seaside because we went by train from Newcastle Central Railway Station with its fascinating machines for stamping your name on a metal strip or buying a bar of chocolate. This photograph of young trainspotters forty years ago captures some of the magic. One boy lovingly touches the nameplate of Golden Plover. Short trousers are the order of the day for younger boys and the older boy wears his school uniform even though it is the weekend. Now, there are leisure clothes and the modern counterparts of these boys would be wearing fashionable clothes. (Dorothy Rand)

My two nieces taken on the fiftieth anniversary of VE Day. Everybody in our street dressed up and joined in a truly fantastic party celebration. It was a day filled with laughter, singing and remembrance of those who were lost in the war. My two nieces stood proud knowing the true reason behind VE Day. (Brian John Hafner)

Me and two friends on Striding Edge, Helvellyn, in 1955. Not quite like climbing Mount Everest, but a good test of stamina nevertheless. That's me on the left, Les in the middle (now in Australia) and Tony on the right (who died a few years ago). How time changes things. (Ronald Pears)

This is World Fitness Endurance record holder Paddy Doyle. He achieved his ninety-seventh fitness endurance record in the Wimbledon half marathon in 1998. So far he has gained fourteen entries into various editions of the *Guinness Book of World Records*. His aim is to achieve 100 national, European and world fitness title records before the millennium. (Mr D. Clifton)

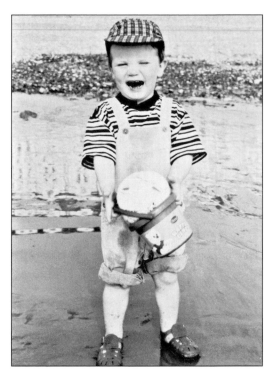

Our son Harry, aged 2, on his first trip to the beach at Eastbourne, August 1998. To me, it reflects the timeless joy brought by a day at the seaside and could almost have been taken in any year of the twentieth century. (Lisa Derighetti)

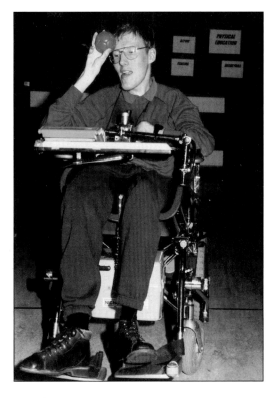

Nicholas attends Hereward College of Further Education in Coventry, which is the national integrated college for students with physical and sensory impairments. Nicholas is pictured playing 'Boccia' (roman bowls) and is the 1999 England and Wales champion. Nicholas will soon be qualified to referee the sport. I took the photograph as part of a major photographic documentary of Hereward students and their lives during the 1998/99 academic year. I presented the images in a book – *Living and Learning at Hereward College*, as well as an exhibition at the college. (Russell Gill)

I like this photo. You don't see many Year 2 pupils dressed like this at school today! The teacher said a lot of photos brought in had no details to say what they were but at least I know the date of this one! The boys look smart and happy and I like the berets and the heavy warm coats. Santa's fashion has never changed! I don't think people dress children as sensibly today. (Lisa Ferguson St Teresa's RC Primary School, **Primary School Winner**)

This photo shows me, aged 5, all dressed up in red, white and blue, with my doll's pram transformed into a coach with my favourite doll made into the Queen. I was ready to attend the local village children's party to celebrate the Coronation of Queen Elizabeth at Lake, Isle of Wight, in 1953. (Patricia Coward)

My dad in about 1914 enjoying a day's holiday from underground in the mines of the Rhondda Valley. He'd travelled to Weston-super-Mare in the steamer from Cardiff and here he is resplendent in his straw boater, white shirt with stiff starched collar, knitted tie with tie pin, waistcoat, dark coat and grey trousers. So different from today's fashions – shorts and a T-shirt. (Gwyneth Birkenshaw)

Our grandchildren wanted to celebrate the anniversary of VE Day and needed a Union flag. Lee and Sinead cut up an old blanket and nailed it to a wooden pole they found on the beach. Using a lipstick and a marker pen, they made their flag. This picture could be of children playing patriotically in the Second World War or at the present time. It has pride of place on our wall. Seeing it gives us hope for the future. (Norman Pascoe)

This photo of me was taken in 1918 in East Molesey, when I was 3. To the best of my memory, it was Peace Day 1918, but as my mother has been dead for over seventy years, I cannot be sure of the occasion. My parents were keen on collecting for the care of wounded soldiers so it could have been a hospital flag day. I remember our glass house where the grapes grown were taken to the local hospital. (Joan Syrett)

In the 1950s, cycle speedway was popular with teenage boys. This is a photo of Dennis Palmer and Colin Egan in the Rider's Individual Championship at Freezy Water, Enfield. They rode for Clay Hill Aces, and as a pair for Enfield. There were about six tracks in Enfield at the time. In 1950, a speedway test match was held at the Empress Hall, Earls Court. England played Holland, and Holland won by 49 points to 47. The photo was in the *Enfield Gazette*. (C.J. Egan)

This is my friend Cliff Church. He is a snowboarding coach and an avid skateboarder. Skateboarding is a relatively new sport compared to a sport like football or cricket and is evolving and growing quickly. Future skateboarders will be able to look back and view the sport in its infancy. (Matthew Hillier)

your town

I took this picture in Blackburn in 1979 while visiting a friend. My attention was focused on the architecture and heritage of the place, terraced houses and steep cobbled streets, when I turned into this particular street. For me, it was so incongruous, a traditional part of English working-class heritage, but repopulated with characters from another culture, another country. These feelings were not negative ones. I welcome the racial and cultural mix that has given strength, invention and colour to our society. However, it still remains a reflection of the changing face of Britain in the twentieth century. (Alan Sams, **Winner**)

When I see bluebells, it takes me back to childhood and early teens, when my late father used to take me and my brothers and sisters walking in the countryside, pointing out all the different flowers, trees, bushes, birds, etc. and the vast fields of bluebells. It looked like a sea of glimmering deep blue. Unfortunately, like my beloved father who would have been 100 years old this year, bluebells have vanished in many places, to mine and the world's loss. Today when I see bluebells, it brings back fond and precious memories. The world's population should try to preserve beauty, not destroy it. (Ann Pope, **Runner Up**)

My mother taught these children at Upper Highgate Infants School in Birmingham. The May Festival seems to have been an annually celebrated event which in 1928 focused on dancing around the Maypole. I like the way this photo shows the incongruity of a traditionally rural custom taking place in an inner city playground. My mother married eight years later. She had to give up her career at that point because in those days married women were not allowed to teach. (Gill Barfield, **Runner Up**)

The car boot sale has become part of the weekly routine during the 1980s and '90s. Probably more people regularly attend such events each Sunday morning than attend church. In the future, there will obviously be the physical evidence of twentieth-century religion, but of car boot sales, only anecdotal and photographic evidence may remain. While not entirely approving of their consumerism, I think they have had a significant effect on our way of life. This photo was taken in late October 1997 at Lewes, East Sussex. (Brian Stephen, **Winner**)

Veal crates were banned in Britain on the grounds of cruelty. But farmers could still export the animals in European crates. When the trade came to the tiny port of Brightlingsea in Essex in 1995, whole families took the Colne Road to prevent the lorries from passing through. After ten months and 600 arrests, the Brightlingsea protesters won the day. The vast majority of protesters were from the town and had never protested about anything in their lives. The historic value is that this marked a new type of 'middle-class' protester, i.e. housewives, shopkeepers, librarians, grandmothers, Scouts, Girl Guides etc. (Nicky Lewin, **Runner Up**)

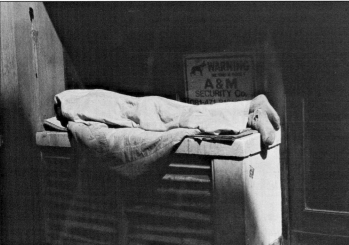

I took this picture last year, as our surroundings change all the time, but I wanted to take photographs that show things as they are, whether it be good or bad. I was born in the East End of London and know it has always been a poor area. It may seem sad to show the negative, but when I saw how the ray of sunshine fell upon him, it made me think that with the new millennium, maybe there will be a 'ray of hope' for homeless people wherever they may be. (Rosie Curran, **Winner**)

Traffic on Tower Bridge in 1950. You rarely see horses and carts any more, except perhaps the odd rag and bone man. This is a pity, in a way, as there was less pollution in the atmosphere. (Jack Terresfield, **ntl Winner**)

This photo shows two gay friends of mine and was taken at Gay Pride in 1996. I believe that this photo is important because it was the twentieth century that gave gay people in Britain, so far, the most rights in history. (Oliver Fritz, **Runner Up**)

At the age of 8 I was given my first camera, which had belonged to my father. After three months, I became quite proficient and took what were considered very decent snaps, which made me determined to become a photographer. The closest I got to this was to become a photographic librarian. My love of London, its buildings and history prompted me to take a unique shot of Nelson's statue including a self-portrait when the monument was cleaned in 1972. (Robert Broeder, **Runner Up**)

This is Daz. He is a 20-year-old displaced person who, with his dog Cabbage, sleeps rough on the historic streets of Nottingham. To me, this photograph represents how little certain aspects of society have changed. From the time of Robin Hood, through to Charles Dickens and up to now, the advent of a new millennium, it is distressing to witness the continued existence of an underclass of fellow human beings. Daz is not a reminder of times present. He is living proof of times past, and if we are not careful, of times future. (Stephen Kornreich-Gelissen, **Runner Up**)

Compton Dunton, near Street in Somerset, in the 1960s. These cottages were destroyed by fire in 1972 and were replaced by modern slated buildings. The thatching is the work of the Wright family, who live in the village and continue a family tradition in the trade which goes back several hundred years. They harvested their own straw. (C. Pursey, **Runner Up**)

These are two retired teachers who nurtured the development of our town's schoolgirls. It was taken in 1990, at the thirty years reunion of Kidderminster High School for Girls class of 1960. Mrs Calaway, right, science teacher, taught reflection and refraction with pins, mirrors and lenses. Mrs Bernie Crossland, a much loved, motherly first form mistress, taught geography. Her past was unsuspected by us at school. She told recent media interviews of being the last surviving suffragette. She joined the Votes for Women movement, aged 7, in 1914 and marched with her mother in Preston, Lancashire, where men pelted her with vegetables. (Joan Margaret Page, **Winner**)

Roundway Hospital in Devizes, Wiltshire, was opened in 1851 as an asylum for the mentally ill. In its heyday, it had as many as 1,411 in-patients. Once admitted, many never returned home. Some outlived their relatives and, even if fit for discharge, had no home to return to. The hospital became their home until they died. Some stayed even after death, buried in the hospital cemetery. The photograph was taken in August 1998 after the hospital had shut down and was being refurbished as private flats. Long-term institutionalisation has become largely obsolete – the new hospital has only seventy-five beds. (Barbara Fuller, **Runner Up**)

While living in Nottingham and working as a postman in the 1980s, I bought an old panoramic camera (basically just a box with a swivelling lens) to make a record of the areas where I delivered. Personally, this is my favourite photo, because I had a friend who lived in these flats; historically, because they've since been demolished and as a warning to future generations, not to trust architects! The billboard is a bonus! (Michael Copsey, **Runner Up**)

My father took me to one of the main streets in the East End of the city to watch the parade of the various trams used throughout the century by Glasgow Corporation Transport. This would be the last time trams would run through the streets of Glasgow. The large crowds which lined the route showed how popular this form of transport had been. I was then aged 13, and this was one of my first photographs. The darkening skies and the gloomy drizzle added to the air of nostalgia and also made an acceptable photograph difficult to achieve. (G.J. Macfarlane, **Runner Up**)

Michael was one of many homeless individuals who would frequent the Old Market area of Bristol; some became alcoholics. Apparently Michael had a good background but was separated from his family. He was vague and mentally maladjusted and could be found with his violin repeatedly crossing the road regardless of traffic. He was not a very good violinist, and posed for me on several occasions. I was distressed to learn that he died from hypothermia in a shop doorway one night. I hope the plight of the homeless in the future will be only history. (Ray Kennedy, **Runner Up**)

I took this picture of a field of poppies in Framwellgate Moor, Durham City, in July 1993, on the day the earth mover seen by the hedge to the right of the picture was brought in to level the field for development. The poppies soon were no more, and the whole area is now covered with houses. Surely a moment in history. (John MacWilliam, **Runner Up**)

The Chief Constable of Bolton with the CID in about 1908. In those days, detectives had to wear bowler hats on duty or top hats for special occasions. Rear second left is my grandfather, James Clegg, who retired as Detective Inspector commanding the CID in March 1926. Four months earlier, he arrested the last Bolton murderer to be executed. On retirement, he was offered a large sum of money for his memoirs, but refused as he did not wish to bring unpleasant memories to people he had met. (Robert Holden, **Runner Up**)

This is a photograph of me and my aunt Dolly at the Bryn Gates Methodist Sunday School Walking Day. It was taken forty-five years ago when I was only 5. The chapel had a walking day every year until 1998 when it stopped because there were not enough children attending Sunday School. This photograph brings fond memories of happy days and reflects how parish communities are a bygone era of faithful people with one goal in mind: to do good and help each other. (Teresa Quinn, **Runner Up**)

The remains of Lesmahagow Priory. The priory was founded in 1144 by the monks from Kelso Abbey. King David first gave the land to the monks. The priory was burnt down in 1335 because the monks were thought to have supported William Wallace and Robert the Bruce in the Scottish Wars of Independence. In 1561 the priory was burnt down again for the Reformation. The parish church was destroyed and re-built in 1803. It is important to keep visual records of the priory because it is a big part of the history of Lesmahagow. (Euan Bennie, **Runner Up**)

This was taken on 10 June 1999. It was the first and last time this century that my teenage children were eligible to vote in a European election. Historically it was the first time the UK engaged in a European election under a system of proportional representation – although in Cardiff only 24 per cent of the electorate actually voted. Britain is likely to forge even closer ties with Europe in the future – tomorrow's voters may be surprised to learn of the political apathy that existed towards Europe at the end of the twentieth century. (Vic Tadd, **Runner Up**)

This is a picture of what was left of the Astoria Cinema in Pokesdown, Bournemouth, May 1999. I went there in the 1960s to see *Dr No* – the first Bond movie. This was a real cinema – one of the many in Bournemouth where you could stay in through continuous performances with two films, a cartoon and Pathé news and hear people say 'this is where we came in, dear'. Over the years, many were turned into bingo halls and, like the one shown, demolished to make way for houses on the site. (Chris Wilson, **Runner Up**)

This is a photograph of flats about to be demolished in my home town of Liverpool. When they were built, they were 'luxury' flats because they had their own bathrooms with running water. They were built in the early 1920s to house families from overcrowded areas. There was also a recreational area where there was a park for children to play in. I think it will be of interest to future generations to see how past housing estates were, back then. (Paula O'Hara, **Runner Up**)

When the Hoylandswaine annual church outing left the village on their horse-drawn waggonettes in 1918, a photographer was there to record the scene. The 'trippers' were accompanied by friends and relatives to the outskirts of the village where they waved their goodbyes. The photographer took one last shot of a group who certainly do not look too disheartened at being left behind. (Cynthia Dillon, **Runner Up**)

Harlow New Town was one of the first new towns developed after the war and I was, at the age of 20, their first Carnival Queen, chosen by the late David Nixon and crowned by the Chief of Harlow Development Corporation, W.W.E. Adams. Harlow was made up of people of various cultural, economic and ethnic backgrounds all working together for the good of the community at large. For many of us Harlow had given us our first house; many like us had come from a couple of rooms in and around London. Communities then worked together instead of pulling themselves asunder. (Mrs Rita Brown – photograph taken by *Harlow Citizen* newspaper, 1954, **Winner**)

The local hairdressers' in my home town of Syston, just outside Leicester. They have a special senior citizens' day where most of the clients are regulars who meet for a good chinwag, although it doesn't show here. If it weren't for the *Woman's Own* magazine and the image of the modern haircut on the wall, this scene I feel would not look out of place in the 1960s. (Martin Patrick Lane, **Runner Up**)

Audrey Grout has been the lollipop lady in my street for more than twenty-seven years and has received a special award from Sir Paul Condon for services to the community. She is now crossing a second generation of children, getting them safely to and from Berrymede School on the South Acton Estate. These days with more and more people driving their children to school, the need for lollipop people isn't so great. I think this photograph of Audrey will remind people of their schooldays when everyone used to walk to their local schools. (Gill Mathias, **Runner Up**)

This photograph shows me aged 18 in 1963. I had arrived in London to sample the 'swinging sixties' and to conquer the city with my charm, sophistication and wit! I was of course a very unsophisticated girl from Gosport, Hampshire, and I spent the first six months with my mouth open in astonishment. However, I did get to Carnaby Street and I adored the fashions. When I travelled home to Gosport and caught the Gosport Ferry, all conversation ceased and all eyes were upon me – it was wonderful! (Lynda Keld, **Winner**)

The photograph, taken in March 1947, depicts the winter with the deepest snowfall this century. We were living in Woodmancote in the Cotswold Hills at the time. Our house is visible over the top, whilst the tiny figures of my mother, sister and myself are dwarfed by the height of the snow. The hamlet was cut off for two weeks, and food and essential supplies had to be brought in on sledges. The snow remained until April, when the thaw set in disclosing spring flowers in bloom beneath. (Christine Carswell, **Runner Up**)

'Over the sea to Skye' in the early '50s required a bit more driving skill than the journey today. Apart from half of the journey taking place over single track roads, negotiating the ferry itself required a Jackie Stewart precision to avoid damaging your car when boarding the ferry with guidance from the ferry crew. However, crossing a modern bridge has removed a lot of the 'magic' of travelling to Skye. (Charles McKirdy, **Runner Up**)

This little chapel was sited in a mining village in Scotland. In 1964 the colliery closed, the village was bulldozed and the residents moved away. In the late 1950s my auntie was married here. Just before the service a bottle of whisky was rolled up the aisle, obviously to give the groom courage! With the demise of the community this unusual tradition died, but it made this wedding unforgettable. A party which lasted for three weeks followed, during which even the priest had too much to drink; he danced on a table singing 'Paddy McGinty's Goat'. What a wedding! (Charlotte Polland, Castle Rock High School, **Secondary School Winner**)

This is a photo of Her Majesty's Yacht *Britannia* during her paying off and decommissioning ceremony when she returned to Portsmouth for the last time on 22 November 1997. The photo was taken from the top of a block of flats on the Gosport side of Portsmouth Harbour. I think this has great historic value as this could be the last in the line of the royal yachts. The photo is very personal to me because in my seven and a half years in the Royal Navy, this is the ship I most wanted to serve on. (Mark Jones)

Some sixty-five years ago, I was a member of Liverpool Amateur Photographic Association. During a tour around our city centre for our annual competition, I came across this delightful scene. I requested them to hold hands as bosom friends with this result. Then came the caption. I thought of three: 'Love at First Sight', 'Our First Acquaintance' and 'Underneath the Arches'. I chose the first one, and won a prize, which I cannot remember, it was so long ago! I reckon that if the two are still alive, they will be in their late 60s by now. (Jim Gonzales, **Runner Up**)

In 1987 there was a great storm that blew many trees down. It had compensations, as it gave better views from some of the hilltops, and those who studied roots at Kew Gardens were delighted to be able to study the upturned roots without them having caused the damage. This photograph of my husband John was taken in Bushey Park, the morning after the Great Storm of 16 October 1987. There was also a hurricane in Bushey Park in June 1908. (Geraldine Mitchell)

This picture was taken by me in 1985 of the free passenger ferry that crosses the Thames at Woolwich, London. I took the picture the year that the GLC was disbanded. So, although these great ferries still run, they no longer carry the badge 'GLC WORKING FOR LONDON'. (David Burrows)

My dad's house during the winter I was born. The year is 1947, but we do not know what the date is precisely. The snow was so deep my grandad had to climb in the window to get in, as you can see. My dad says the snow blocked the firewood my grandparents had left outside and they had to make do with as little as possible. (Geraint Davies)

Princess Diana's coffin being driven to her final resting place. I travelled to London on that fateful day of Saturday 6 September 1997 with my stepson; everyone will remember that day in history for a long time to come. The atmosphere everywhere was of disbelief, but mostly I recall the hushed silence. I remember distinctly the horses hooves clip-clopping in the silence when at first she was taken to the service, Elton John's haunting 'Candle in the Wind' and just at that moment the wind blowing: heartbreaking history is made. (Lynne Torson)

This picture shows Leigh-on-Sea, Essex. The cockle boat in the foreground being unloaded is the *Renown*. She is owned by the family who have fished for cockles for generations. An earlier *Renown* was one of the small ships that went to Dunkirk to rescue British soldiers from the beaches. During this operation, the *Renown* was bombed and sunk, killing her crew – which included members of the family who owned her. Brave men indeed. (Roy S. Smith)

This street of terraced houses in Sincil Street, Lincoln, long ago converted into small shops, was between an old factory behind them on the left and the Market Hall which still stands on the right. Some of the shops have been destroyed to give access to the new bus station which replaced the factory, and the rest are due to be demolished soon. Those are among the oldest shop buildings in the city and some of the last family businesses in the country. (Roger Minshull)

This picture was taken in August 1998 from the top of St Andrews Street in Bordesley Green. It shows a stunning August sunset, silhouetting the Birmingham city centre from Broad Street to Birmingham University, showing the Rotunda and the BT Tower. (Robert O'Neill)

This is the last of four Trident submarines built at Barrow-in-Furness. With the cold war ending the town is struggling to come to terms with a reduction in the workforce from 14,000 down to 5,000, due to concentrating for one decade on one type of ship. Many sub-contracting firms closed down, house prices fell and the future looked bleak. Then a corner was turned, partly because of massive European and Government grants but mostly because of the spirit of the local people. The yard received orders for several surface ships and we all look forward to the new Millennium. (Norman Pascoe)

I spent three years as a mature student in Middlesbrough studying photography. This shot was taken in 1996 and features two buskers playing the Beatles' 'Please Please Me'. I returned to this spot several days later to give them a copy of the photograph but unfortunately found no trace of them. From a personal point of view, the photograph represents the start of a new career direction and how my style of photography changed during my time as a degree student. Wherever I've travelled, I've always considered buskers a welcome addition to the character of a town. (Trevor Chaytor)

The 'Angel of the North' was erected amid much publicity on the southern outskirts of Gateshead in 1998 and I was there to see and photograph it being assembled. Distinctive and enigmatic, it will outlive its early critics and admirers and is expected to survive well into the next millennium. (Trevor Ermel)

Bridlington beach, summer 1983. It is one of those pictures that could have been taken at any time in England since the '30s. The only details hinting at a rough dating are the swimming trunks. Families, including mine, continue to holiday on the 'Yorkshire Riviera'. (Michael Pearson)

While walking in the rain at Stratford-on-Avon (fortunately with a ready camera), I snapped this couple enjoying a typical British fish 'n' chips meal. What a pleasant way to make the best of inclement weather! (Mr Willoughby Gullachsen)

Croag Patrick, County Mayo, Ireland, summer 1981. It was taken during the annual pilgrimage to Ireland's Holy Mountain. I can remember black flags flying at the base of the Republican hunger strikers. The pilgrimage continues, as it has for centuries, and will hopefully outlast the troubles. (Michael Pearson)

In autumn 1960 my youngest sister was 10 years old and still shorter than me. We lived in Penarth, South Glamorgan. The pillar she is standing on was once in front of a kiosk where my great-aunt used to buy me ice cream until I was about 5 years old (in 1945). By 1960 the kiosk had disappeared over the cliff. Last year when I was there with my husband, the cliffs had eroded further. The railings were now in front of where the pillar once stood! (Angela Robinson)

This picture brings back many memories of a man who in the 1980s still lived as he had since the early 1900s – no electricity, drainage or hot water and still using an earth toilet. His rented farm is approximately 100 yards from a main road linking Sheffield to the east coast, not high up on the Yorkshire Moors. My contact with Bernard was through being the farm agent's property repairer. Though life must have been grim, Bernard could still tell a tale and raise a smile. I will always remember entering his house to be greeted by the blazing Yorkshire range. (G. Snuggs)

While resting in our hotel room on holiday in Carlisle in 1994, I heard music. This was the splendid scene unfolding beneath our windows. It was the colourful but poignant last Carlisle Parade of the Regimental Band of the King's Own Border Regiment who were being moved from Carlisle Castle to Catterick Barracks, Yorkshire. The building is the sixteenth-century old Town Hall. (Helen Harris)

The Runcorn Widnes Transporter bridge with St Mary's Church in the background just before it was demolished to make way for the new Road Bridge. I took the picture in 1960. It brings back memories to me because as a 15-year-old office boy I used to cross on the transporter twice a day from West Bank Power Station Widnes to ICI Runcorn. It cost 2d to cross the Transporter. This picture will bring back many memories to the people of Widnes and Runcorn. (Mr J.G. Sparks)

This photograph was taken outside the Millennium Dome in Holyrood, Edinburgh, in July 1999. The people in the photograph are visitors to Scotland's most exciting Visitors' Centre. The Dome hosts 'Our Dynamic Earth'. This is a journey of discovery that takes you from the very beginning of time to the unknown future we call home. I live in the Royal Mile (Edinburgh). I can see the Dome from my window. I've watched the Dome being built step by step and have taken more photographs. (Sam McIntyre)

When John Lennon was assassinated in New York in December 1980, the shock waves could be felt around the world, and nowhere more so than his home town, Liverpool. In this photograph taken ten years after his death, Lennon admirer Jayne Tunnicliffe visits the graffiti-covered gates of a former Salvation Army children's home in Liverpool's Woolton district. The leafy grounds of the home were among Lennon's favourite childhood haunts and he immortalised it in the 1967 Beatles song – 'Strawberry Fields Forever'. Today, it remains a popular tourist destination where Beatles fans can experience the evocative place that inspired the song. (Jayne Tunnicliffe)

This is a photo of me in front of the Skylon at the Festival of Britain Exhibition in 1951. I had never been away from home and this was my first ever trip to London. I was so excited and overawed by it all and we covered everything in one day. All I remember today is the Skylon and sniffing perfume from each corner of the world though I can only bring to mind 'spices from the Far East'. After the long years of the war it was all magical. (Maureen Lawther)

Two of the last few remaining true Romany horse-drawn caravans which spent a couple of days in my village in late May, on their way to Appleby New Fair – a traditional annual event. The man came to my house to ask for drinking water. In an age when speed seems to be an all-consuming passion, these two small vans with their occupants and drivers, whose horses quietly grazed on the opposite side of the road, seemed momentarily to bring time to a welcome standstill. (Patricia Howe)

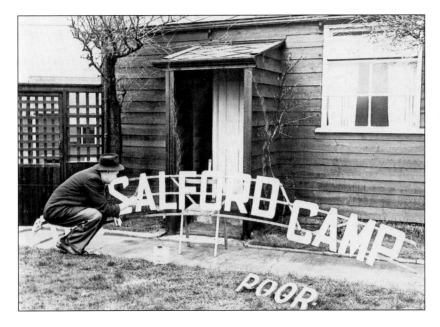

This picture taken in April 1954 shows superintendent 'Uncle' George Livesey making ready for another busy season at the Salford Poor Children's Holiday Camp, Prestatyn, North Wales. The camp, which was opened in 1928, helped to alleviate the poverty, hardships and chronic disabilities of many thousands of boys and girls. One of its original founders was Captain S.H. Hampson OBE, MC, who was the chairman both of the holiday camp and the Royal British Legion when this photograph was taken. My father who visited the camp as a child appreciated his first view of the British coastline and benefited immensely. (Bill Wilkinson)

This picture comes from a series on football clubs. It shows some York City players changing before a match against Colchester United in October 1983. They won 5–1 and went on to win that season's Fourth Division championship with a record number of points. The player by the window sharing a joke is John Byrne who was later transferred to Queens Park Rangers and played international football for the Republic of Ireland in their glory days under Jack Charlton. (Michael Pearson)

Marske Hall was built in 1625 as a residence for William Pennyman Esquire. In 1755 it was acquired by the Dundas family, becoming the home of the Marquis of Zetland. When the Dowager Marchioness died, it was no longer required. With great forethought, a local villager, Susan Sidaway, proposed it as a Leonard Cheshire Home and it has remained so for thirty-six years, caring for disabled residents. Charles Dickens visited Marske to see the three unusual stone turrets. There was a mulberry tree in the centre of the lawn from 1932 to 1939 and there was Maypole dancing and the crowning of a May Queen here. (Vera Robinson MBE)

The annual Notting Hill Carnival. This vibrant festival has gone on for years and is one of the biggest events in London. (Percy Wilding)

I took this picture back in 1991 when I first started learning photography. The subject is Anne McDonagh. She has lived all her life on the streets, in and around Birmingham. I met her one Sunday morning – she was a forlorn figure, but very friendly and easy to communicate with. The image is strong, but that is reflected only by her surroundings. I feel that as we approach the end of the century, images like these can be seen in all cities. I would like to see this kind of existence eradicated as we move into the next century. (Patrick James Isaac)

Taken in 1951, when my wife and I spent a week in London during the Festival of Britain, this photograph shows the Dome of Discovery. For Peter Mandelson, substitute Herbert Morrison: it makes our Millennium version seem passé. (Alan Smith)

This is Morrison Street, Edinburgh, in the 1960s when Beatlemania was all the rage. The Regal in Lothian Road was to be the concert venue. It was decided that a queue for tickets would have to be formed – consequently girls demanded to be allowed to sleep on the pavement. In the local press, many people wrote that parents who allowed them to sleep out in a rowdy area should be prosecuted. The girls got their own way as the council provided toilets and parents provided food and drinks. I'm sure the girls who slept out thought it was worthwhile. (Francis McCormack)

I took this photo when I went on a photography course going around Portsmouth Football Club's ground. While walking round I met some young boys who live near the stadium. It was taken when Pompey were celebrating their centenary. It will give future generations an insight into Portsmouth's own club that has survived for a hundred years and deserves to for another hundred or more. (Kate Baverstock, Springfield School)

On Saturday 6 March 1999, the River Derwent burst its banks: one of the villages that was flooded was Elvington, where I live. My house is on the main road where the flood was. As you can see, we had a roadblock right outside our house to stop cars going through. The only way you could get to the shop was to wear wellies and walk very close to the kerb. We had to have sandbags delivered. There were TV reporters about nearly all the time. People were canoeing in the water. The flood lasted about a week and left behind a lot of dirt. (Hannah Foster, Fulford School)

St Augustine's Church in Hedon, which is known as the King of Holderness. I always try to include as much as possible in my photos. In this one, the church is behind lots of leaves and trees which makes an excellent foreground for it. The Cubs, Brownies, Scouts and general public go there for services, to meet and have a good time. My 8-year-old sister Kathryn plays the violin for the orchestra. The church is very important to Hedon and its people. (Matthew Lees, Hedon County Primary)

war

This photograph shows two survivors of the 'forgotten' Burma campaign of the Second World War at the 1995 VJ Day parade in London – the fiftieth anniversary of the conflict's end. Outside Buckingham Palace were veterans from all the services, the Royal Family, the Prime Minister, and thousands of spectators. My father served with the Gurkhas during the war years and like the subjects of this picture received the Burma Star medal. I cried when the Kohima epitaph was read – 'When you come home, tell them of us and say for your tomorrow we gave our today.' (Alex Stanhope, **Runner Up**)

This photo reminds us of the work women did during the First World War. It is my grandpa's great-aunt, Mini Stuart, who worked at the Royal Infirmary, Glasgow. She helped to nurse wounded soldiers coming back from the war. It was the valuable contribution of women like Mini that got them the vote in 1918. She also had an interesting link with the Second World War – she had a summerhouse in Largs and my grandpa was evacuated there during the war. So she helped in two world wars. She died in 1955 so this photo survives as an important record of her. (Kirsty Thomson, Duncanrig Secondary School, **Secondary School Winner**)

I took this photograph in Flanders, Belgium, in 1995. It is of the Menin Gate, Ypres. My grandfather fought and was wounded at Ypres, so this picture is of great interest to me. To try to capture the atmosphere of the place, I used photographs I had taken of a war memorial in Glasgow. The negatives were sandwiched together in the darkroom, producing this photograph – one of a series called the 'Ghosts of Flanders'. (Jim McCann, **Runner Up**)

India was considered to be the jewel in the British Empire's crown until her independence on 15 August 1947. The air base in Ambala was the home to 28 AC Squadron of the RAF, who often flew sorties over the Himalayas. The photograph, taken by my grandfather, Warrant Officer Maurice Lowrey, portrays the inspection of the squadron's Hawker Audaxes. It is fair to say that the regimental imagery of this photograph, which was taken in 1938, portrays the organisation and efficiency that has been symbolic of the RAF since its formation on 1 April 1918. (Nicholas Moran, **Runner Up**)

My great-great-grandfather, Colour Sergeant Charles Cadogan Edwards, is pictured outside Chester Castle. The year was 1915 and, as Recruiting Sergeant, he was responsible for enlisting volunteers to fight in the First World War. Charlie was well known by locals as the tallest man in Chester. At 6 ft 6 in he certainly looks the part here, surrounded by posters of Lord Kitchener summoning the troops. This photograph will show future generations that past members of the Chester community were prepared to go to war for the good of their country. (Miss I. Bacon, **Runner Up**)

My grandmother with her brother, Rhodri Owen Jones, and her father. They are sitting in their garden near Bala during the First World War, during Rhodri's final leave from his regiment. He died at Passchendaele in 1916, demonstrating the use of a mortar bomb to his regiment, and was awarded the Victoria Cross. His face reflects an inner knowledge of war; his sister and father are anxious outsiders reading the news and asking questions to gain an impression. During this century our perception of war has become more immediate, through on the spot TV, but also more remote using hi-tech weaponry. (Ruth Sayers, **Runner Up**)

This photo, taken in September 1914 by a Hastings beach photographer, shows an English family posing with soldiers convalescing from wounds probably received at Mons. The little girl on the right is my Auntie Zoë. The war was still popular with the public who encouraged children to befriend the Tommies and treat them as heroes. The soldiers, not family members, show different emotions. The artilleryman (front left) seems embarrassed. His cigarette tucked behind his ear, he looks away from the camera maybe seeing what future generations have yet to grasp. The Somme and Passchendaele were still to come. (Stu Morrison, **Winner**)

My great-grandfather in 1915 during the First World War. He was German and won a medal for bravery. He was also Jewish and that's why he wasn't allowed to wear a hat with a spike. Sadly in the Second World War he and my great-grandmother died when taken by Hitler and his crew. She was gassed and he became ill in the camp called Belsen. (Joe Yoffe, Parrswood High School, **Secondary School Winner**)

I think this image captures a moment in time superbly. On knowing the date and seeing the time on Big Ben, it is a definite moment recorded on film. All the people standing still add to the sense of occasion. It was taken by my friend, Matt Partridge. It marks the end of the First World War, seventy years ago to the minute. (Jules Thom, **Runner Up**)

This is a picture of me taken at Queen's Hospital for children in Hackney in 1943. My father was the ENT surgeon here. Nightly, German bombers dropped their bombs over London. Every evening we had to take the children and babies down into the basement along with bedpans and bottles of milk among the cockroaches! The stiff collars and cuffs we had to wear were most impractical and chafed our necks red raw. In the 1990s the hospital, renamed The Queen Elizabeth, was closed, taking with it memories of the war and of all who worked within its walls. (Nancy Vlasto, **Runner Up**)

VE Day at the end of the Second World War. My grandad is in the picture, with all his friends who lived in his street. After all the rationing they had to put up with, it was great to have a slap-up feast and decorate the street with bunting. It was also a time to reflect, to think about all the people killed during the war. Some children had lost their families, which was very sad. But they knew it was all over now, and they hoped and prayed for better times. (Lucy Crew, Dunottar School, **Secondary School Winner**)

My father, Gunner G. Hazell, facing, was one of the first wounded to be evacuated from the D-Day landings in Caen, 1944. He had one leg amputated. Also in the photo are Pte. A.W. Harris and Sister M. Melland (Roehampton Hospital). I was 4 and vividly remember visiting Roehampton. The grounds were full of amputees. I watch television today and see yet another war raging and wonder why history repeats itself. My hope for future generations is the abolition of all wars. My father died at 58. His cancer had begun where his leg was amputated. (Mrs J.A. Pike, **Runner Up**)

The Lancaster bomber of the Battle of Britain Memorial Flight as it flew over Derwent Dam on the fiftieth anniversary of the Dambuster raids on 16 May 1993. This flypast was a tribute paid to the men who took part in this mission to destroy the Ruhr dams in Germany, led by Wing Commander Guy Gibson. Many of the remainder of the participating aircrew were there by the Derwent Dam on this day to take this salute, and many thousands of people travelled there to witness it. It was a great tribute to courageous airmen. (David Smith, **Runner Up**)

After the Second World War had been on for a while, we decided to open our hallowed portals to the troops and war workers. At first, they were slow to appear, but once they did and found we were a group of 18 year olds and over, they came in droves. We had to make a rota for serving teas and sandwiches, no sliced bread and yellow rock cakes. We held sports, plays and dances, with a wind-up gramophone and six records. Such simple pleasures; we had such fun in such hard times. Some romances led to marriage, including my own sisters, still together. (Joan Songhurst, **Runner Up**)

This is me being carried by a fireman after our home had been destroyed by a doodlebug (a flying bomb) during the Second World War. It first appeared in the *Daily Mirror* when they were appealing for homes for the homeless. Soon after, I was evacuated.
I was billeted with an elderly couple who were very kind. I was very homesick. We had strict food rationing and we needed clothing coupons to buy clothes. There was so much rejoicing when peace came. We had a street party for VE Day that I'll never forget. (Eileen Alexander, **Winner**)

This has personal importance because it is a picture of my grandmother in the ack-ack battery in the Second World War. It has historical importance because this was the first ack-ack battery of its kind. In this picture they are making model planes so they know what the planes look like. They are doing this because some of these ladies, including my grandmother, were plane spotters trying to spot planes coming over from Germany. They were based in Wimbledon Common in London to spot the planes coming over to attack London. (Catherine Harrison, Westlands School, **Secondary School Winner**)

I took this photograph in April 1999 when I visited Auschwitz Death Camp in Poland. Here, in the middle of the twentieth century, 1.5 million innocent people were murdered. Most were European Jews, but Russians, Czechs, Gypsies, Poles and many others perished too. They were exterminated because a political idea became more important than human life itself. It is vital that future generations see pictures like this and learn about our past. It is said that he who ignores history is condemned to repeat it – we must ensure that we do not allow this to happen. (Alan Riley, **Runner Up**)

My father, Douglas George Harris, took this photo in 1945 of a victory street party with all the children of Carltoun Street, Kentish Town, taking part. There were flags and bunting across the street and many happy faces, no longer showing the fear and worry of war. At the top of the street are two air raid shelters – one on each side – and the lamp posts are partly painted white so that they could be seen during the blackouts. Carltoun Street was demolished in 1963 during slum clearance and when it was rebuilt with blocks of flats, it was renamed Weedington Road. (Douglas Harris, **Winner**)

This is a photo taken in 1940 of Beccles (Suffolk) Home Guard River Patrol. The Local Defence Volunteers – later renamed Home Guard – organised a patrol of the River Waveney using an ex-holiday cruiser, the *Happy-Go-Lucky*, with a four-man crew armed with First World War rifles and fifty rounds of ammunition. Their task was to patrol the river at night and to rendezvous with another HG boat coming upriver from Oulton Broad. If necessary, they were to engage enemy paratroops and they also had the task of marking any fallen unexploded bombs. This photo shows one four-man crew – my father, Bob Martin (seated front left), Bob Gual (seated right), Billy Thurgar (standing left) and Frank Youell. (Mal Martin, **Runner Up**)

A group of Whirlwind helicopters of 155 Squadron based in Kuala Lumpur in 1956 returning from troop lifting operations in the Malayan jungle. They operated during what was to become known as the Forgotten War between 1948 and 1957 when British and Commonwealth troops withstood the growing surge of Communist soldiers in the Far East. The eventual victory by the Allies was a combination of good tactics and determination over many years. I was a crew member on one of the aircraft and flew many sorties over enemy-held territory. (C.J. Beardwell, **Runner Up**)

I took this photograph in London's Whitehall in 1961 when taking part in a sit-down demonstration against nuclear weapons. This demonstration was organised by the Committee of 100, a group who were part of the Campaign for Nuclear Disarmament (CND), dedicated to non-violent civil disobedience. CND was one of the most important and influential popular movements of the twentieth century, which attracted many thousands of people in Britain. This photo illustrates the public response to the frightening proliferation of nuclear weapons during the Cold War and reminds me of my involvement in the idealism of the time. (Christopher Holden, **Runner Up**)

1100hrs on 2 March 1991, somewhere north-west of Kuwait city. Normally the sky would be a bright baby blue, but not today. The retreating Iraqi army has set fire to the oil wells and it's snowing black soot. The donkey walking off into the distance was weak and forlorn. I got to go home. I wonder if the donkey did too. (Stephen R. McGinnigle, **Runner Up**)

In the early 1990s, I worked as a music journalist. One of my assignments was a rave near Belfast. On the way there, the Irish photographer with me was called by a local paper to cover a riot on the Falls Road. I went with him. As we reached the street shown on the photograph – just one block from Sinn Fein's headquarters – the IRA were hijacking and burning cars, and barricading the street. British Army helicopters were everywhere; troops were being readied. I was in a war zone. As an Englishman, you can imagine how tightly my mouth was shut. (David Fowler, **Runner Up**)

This is a photo of my great-grandad's uncle, Bill Cook. It was taken during the Boer War, the war before the First World War. I think this photo is important to British history because it is of a British soldier who fought in a war one hundred years ago. It also clearly shows the type of uniform soldiers wore then. At this time many people would have been unable to afford to have had a photo taken at a photographic studio. Also very few people had cameras. So I think photos like this one are quite rare. (Emma Cook, Hayes School, Brompton)

This photograph was taken in 1915, which means that all these men freely joined the Army to fight. It tells the story of courage, bravery, loyalty and love for their country. In it is Gus Cohen – a third class passenger, who on 10 April 1912, sailed on the greatest liner of all time – the *Titanic*, which hit an iceberg and never completed her maiden voyage. He was rescued and brought on board the *Carpathia*. He sits on the floor with his cane clasped in his hands and his cap tilted. (Steven Irvin, Drumglass High School)

For some months Father was stationed at the Canadian cavalry depot at Shorncliffe. After the death of a much liked and respected officer, he was asked to arrange a funeral. This he did with such panache (reversed boots in the mount's stirrups, Guard of Honour, gun carriage, last post, volley of shots, etc.) that he was asked for repeats from time to time and nicknamed the 'Undertaker'. 'Not a dry eye on parade', he remarked about the first ceremony. (Colin Reid)

This photograph shows Armistice Day celebrations following the First World War in 1919 on a castle mound in Pembrokeshire, Wales. Included in it are my great-great-grandparents and my great-grandfather and great-grandmother who are still alive today at the age of 94. The Japanese flag is shown supporting the fact that they were our allies in that war. I really like the clothes they are wearing and would like to dress up in them if I could. It is funny to see how many people are wearing hats and how solemn everyone looks. For an Armistice Day celebration they did not look particularly joyful! (Emily Gaskell, St Teilo's Church High School)

My parents' wedding in December 1915 at St George's Church, Handsworth (now a mosque). By this time father had spent some months at the front, been gassed, and returned to this country for recuperation. A dozen of the FGH Sergeants' Mess turned out for the Guard of Honour some of them staying at home for a day or two. My mother said of it that the 'hall seemed full of swords'; my aunt said that the 'house was full of men'. (Colin Reid)

This picture shows the two sides of war – bad and good – the horrible killings and the friendships created by countries joining together against a common enemy. Here is my great-uncle Ernest Crowell (second from the left) who came to England with the United States 8th Air Force to fight in the Second World War. He completed twenty-six extremely dangerous missions as a tail-gunner on B24s and B17s and won many medals before he was killed at 21. Although many millions of Allies died, the Second World War forged an alliance among most of Western Europe which has lasted to this day. (Alec Crowell, Hazlegrove King's Bruton Junior School)

These photos were taken from the album of my great-aunt by marriage, Emmeline Beck née Langford. She is the very tall nurse in the picture on the left. Highfield Hall was a convalescent home for servicemen near Southampton and the pictures were taken in 1917. The theatre had no anaesthetic machine and the men wore the uniform of the wounded, a blue suit with wide lapels of red and white. (Dr Jane Richards)

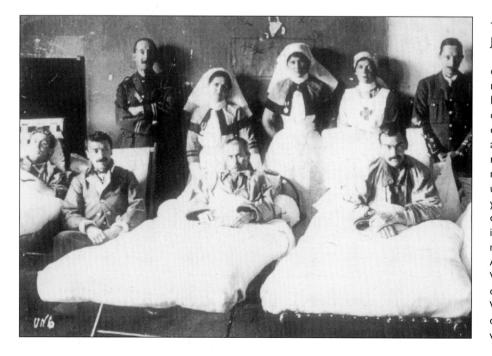

This shows my great-grandfather, James Convery (29 February 1868–22 February 1928), centre, convalescing in a French military hospital during the First World War. Remembered chiefly as a conflict which decimated a generation of boys and young men, the photo reminds us of the contribution made by the middle-aged. An unskilled man, James was 46 years old when war was declared and probably enlisted in the Labour Corps. We may never know this for certain – Army records for the First World War were severely damaged during the Second World War and those not destroyed are too fragile to be viewed. (John Convery)

This is a photograph of my grandfather George Lee (1880–1949). It was taken during the steaming trials of HMS *Iron Duke* in 1913. He was an electrical engineer in Portsmouth Dockyard, and during the First World War he was awarded the MBE for his contribution to restarting the engines of a ship that had broken its moorings and was in danger of running aground. This picture is a reminder of the preparations this country was making during the years leading up to the First World War. (Jacqueline Bedford)

My father, Raymond Briggs, enlisted in the Liverpool Scottish at the age of 19, on 5 August 1914. He had to wait for his father's return from a round trip on a cargo boat before he could obtain permission to enlist, and found that few regiments had vacancies. He is shown wearing a jacket in the foreground of a group in camp at Edinburgh but soon received his uniform. Kilts, however, proved highly unsuitable for trench warfare. Unlike many of the citizen army, he survived to become a professional soldier, commanding an armoured division at Alamein. (Nancy Edwards)

This photograph was taken as night fell on the Somme Valley in the vicinity of the 1 July front line near Beaumont-Hamel. In the foreground is a Celtic cross, while to the rear stands the bronze memorial to the 51st Highland Division who fought bravely in this sector of the battlefield in 1916. The photograph was taken in October 1998 during a visit to the First World War battlefields of France and Belgium – a fascinating and moving experience for anyone with an interest in history. (Iain Cameron)

Robert Dunsire enlisted in January 1915 into the 13th Royal Scots and arrived in France in July that year. Early on 26 September 1915 in the Battle of Loos, he went out of the trenches to the front line. Under heavy fire he rescued a wounded man from behind the firing lines and carried him 76 yds. Later, another man near the German lines was heard shouting for help – Dunsire crawled out with complete disregard for the enemy and carried him to safety. Shortly after, the Germans captured the ground he had covered. On 7 December, he was decorated with the VC by George V at Buckingham Palace. He then returned to the front where he was promoted to Corporal, but sadly he was killed by a trench mortar on 30 January 1916. (George Tullis)

This photograph shows the plaque of surrender. I consider that this photograph may be unique because the wooden plaque shown was constructed, painted and erected by Army Corps engineers on the evening of the surrender of German Forces in North Western Europe to Field Marshal Montgomery on Lüneberg Heath on 4 May 1945. Overnight the plaque was vandalised and destroyed by the German 'Werewolf' underground movement. It is interesting to note that, although the actual surrender took place on 4 May 1945, Europe celebrates annually on 8 May. (Sidney G. Barlow)

My father with a section of the Border Regiment setting up a machine gun emplacement on the North-West Frontier in 1916. He served with the regiment from 1914 to 1919. Also, his age just put him in the regular Fire Service from 1940 to 1947. He died in an accident in 1954, young for such an eventful life. (Ronald Pears)

The caption under this photograph in a family album is 'Off to the War'. It was taken in August 1914 in Ireland where my father, RSM Kyberd of the Royal Field Artillery was stationed. He is seen standing on the right. The men were sent straight to France, leaving their families to return to England alone crossing a very rough Irish Sea. It was five years before my father came home for good. My eldest sister remembers a young private coming to the door and saying 'War has been declared.' (C. Houghton Brown)

One of the frequent landing crashes during the First World War. I am given to understand that more aircraft from what was then known as the 'Air Corps' were lost in this way than in actual combat! (George Brian Kelsall)

This is a photograph of my uncle – Flight Lieutenant Albert Payne. My uncle is in the front, the gentleman in the back is unknown. Born in Barry, Glamorgan, in 1888, my uncle emigrated to Canada in 1907. He joined the 5th Canadian Army in 1915. He fought in France, but was wounded and medically discharged. He then joined the Royal Flying Corps. On 13 January 1918 on a trial flight from Hendon to Ipswich, his plane crashed, burst into flames and he was killed. He was just 30 years old. His remains were interred in his home town of Barry on 25 January 1918 with full military honours. (Albert Lee)

A studio portrait of my grandfather in naval uniform. He was a crew member aboard the battle cruiser *Abuka* which with *Cressy* and another ship were sent forth into the English Channel in August 1914 to lure out the German Navy in the early days of the First World War. Tragically for the crews, a single U-boat dispatched all three ships to the bottom, drowning over a thousand sailors including my grandfather. This took place in the first two weeks of the war and was one of the worst tragedies in modern naval history. (C.J. Beardwell)

This picture is important to me because it is of my great-uncle, Duncan Ross. It was taken in 1941 when he was in the Australian Army. He had gone to Australia as a teenager to escape unemployment and depression at home. He hoped to find a better life. He enlisted during the Second World War. Many people forget that the former colonies still fought on Britain's side in the world wars. The photo is a good reminder of the close links between the motherland and its offspring. (Dawn Magowan, Duncanrig Secondary School)

On 27 September 1941, Bromsgrove and District launched 'Tank Week'. By the purchase of National Saving stamps and certificates from post offices and selling centres, people could help the war effort by saving as much as they could until the war was won. Belbroughton had an indicator showing a baby on the scales and all were asked to watch it grow as the daily total was added. By the end of that week Belbroughton had sold a magnificent total of £13,558 15s of stamps and certificates, approximately £8 per head. The district total was £330,000. (Mrs M.C. Hinton)

This 1943 photo has much historic value and memories for me and should have for thousands of others in the future. The Second World War has always been thought of as a man's time, but people don't realise the part women played. Women did their bit, working in munitions and other essential factories. These women were from a factory at the Pier Pavilion in Herne Bay, which made camouflage netting. At one time, over 200 women worked there. My grandmother is featured in the top right-hand corner. The women were always smiling and making the most of things. I would like others to kindle the fond memories as I am for future generations. (Jessika Bomber, Methodist College, Belfast)

This is a ship I served on – HMS *Albatross*. I was on her from 1942–3 in the Far East. Originally an Australian ship, she was transferred to the RN in 1938 where she stayed until she was broken up in Hong Kong in 1954. (She also helped build Sydney Bridge by winching the centre span into place to great cheers from the onlookers.) Her cranes, which were used to hoist and lower the Walrus aircraft into the water, were a great asset and her planes were used for spotting for the big guns and searching for subs. She served at Madagascar as a depot ship and Normandy where she was hit by a Dackel Torpedo – a 9 knot enemy weapon. It ran straight for 16 miles and then circled for two hours before striking. (Ben Perry)

U 532 being escorted into Gladstone Dock in Liverpool after being captured on the surface. I cannot remember the precise date but it was either late 1944 or early 1945. (Raymond Gill)

A group of 'our boys' from the Second World War standing in front of one of the world's most recognised landmarks. My great-uncle Harold, aged 18, is on the far right. Shortly after this picture was taken he suffered shell shock, was branded a coward and sent to a mental hospital where he remained until he died aged 61. Nowadays, post traumatic stress disorder is widely recognised and fortunately service personnel rarely suffer Harold's fate. (Miss B. Lloyd)

The men in this photo belong to the Duke of Cornwall's Light Infantry. It was taken at their training camp on Bodmin Moor in 1944 just before D-Day; this regiment was part of the 43 Wessex Division. My mother's brother, Joseph Thomas Fisher, aged 22, can be seen standing on the far right of the photo. This regiment was part of XXX Corps – they fought their way through Holland and eventually over Arnhem Bridge. After the war, Uncle Joe spent his life working at the Massey Ferguson tractor plant in Coventry and retired from there in 1985. He is now 78. (P.M. Bassett)

Progress through this century has been greater than at any time during man's existence here on earth – from the invention of the wheel to landing on the moon, from caves to castles. We could go on and on. Man's behaviour to fellow man has not changed – we can still record two world wars and other minor wars in this century. My photograph shows this with three family generations who have played their part in serving in three of them. Much as we must admire the progress in technology and medical science, we still have a lot to learn about human coexistence. (J.J. Perkins)

My dad in 1940 at the end of his aircrew training: he is on the right of the front row. He was then posted to 102 Squadron on Whitleys and then to 35 Squadron on Halifaxes. On 24 July 1941, he was shot down attacking the German battle cruiser, *Scharnhorst*. With three engines on fire and five of the crew wounded, they managed to bale out. Taken prisoner, they spent nearly four years in various prisoner of war camps. (Ian Constable)

This is a photo taken in Poland in 1940 by a German guard to send to his family. We were working on building roads and railways. We did not all get off the beaches at Dunkirk. My war years were spent in prisoner of war camps working twelve hours a day on a small piece of black bread and washy soup. (J.L. Wallis)

I was a member of the crew of a merchant ship, the SS *Clan Macwhirter*, that was torpedoed on 26 August 1942 in the North Atlantic midway between Madeira and the Azores. This photograph was taken by a member of the crew of the Portuguese sloop *Pedro Nunez* that came to our rescue just north of Madeira, after a voyage of 250 miles in five days. This is the last photograph in a series of five, taken in sequence from the first sighting of the boat. (L.S. Webb)

My grandad was a blacksmith and worked for a company called Ogle's. They made machinery for farms. This is a picture of my grandad Albert Bull (left) with a new type of machine they had made. It helped in harvesting corn and wheat – a combine harvester. During the Second World War, we could not bring food into the country on ships as the Germans sank them. These machines were very important in Great Britain so that people would have enough food to eat. As he could not join the soldiers to go away and fight, he joined the Home Guard. (Lauren Blunden, Lammas School)

This is a photo of some German survivors from the *U300* landing at Gibraltar from our ship HMS *Recruit*. We sank the submarine on our way out east in 1945. It is a poignant reminder of the fortunes of war and, in as much as we launched our boats to pick up survivors, to me it was a culminating action. I went on to survive another year of service in the Royal Navy before being demobbed. Incidentally the POWs were blindfolded and given to believe they were being landed in Blighty. (Why? I do not know!) (Ben Perry)

Left: Winston Churchill visiting the troops during the Second World War. It shows a typical Churchillian pose with the hat, cigar and walking stick, but it is not posed for an official photo. It reminds us of the inspiration Churchill gave to people, especially the troops during the Second World War and illustrates the importance of boosting morale in difficult times. (Beverley Reynolds)

Below: This photo captures an important moment in British history, the visit of two inspirational Second World War leaders to motivate the troops (many of whom can be seen in the background). It is significant as it was not taken for propaganda purposes. 'Monty' would have been a familiar face to the Desert Rats but to see two leaders together, each supreme in their own field – Montgomery, the soldier, and Churchill, the statesman, must have been a great boost to morale. Both photographs were taken by my aunt's fiancé who served with the Royal Armoured Corps in North Africa (one of the Desert Rats) and in Italy before being killed during the D-Day landings in 1944. (Ken Reynolds)

Above: This is a picture of me (extreme right), sifting sand, with my mother and young friend at the seaside, early 1940s. All the seaside elements are there – sand, pebbles, sunglasses, swimsuits, sunbathers, a basket with a thermos but what strikes the modern eye is the grim, forbidding (though perhaps reassuring at the time) barricading 'against infection and the hand of war'. Would it really have deterred an invasion? Did it make people feel safer? It obviously didn't spoil my day on the beach. (Janet Capon Neri)

Left: My namesake, Jeanne, in Chamonix, 1946. She was recuperating after being imprisoned in a concentration camp, for being a member of the Belgian Resistance. They helped airmen who were shot down including my father aged 19. He escaped as far as Paris where unfortunately he was arrested by the Gestapo for being a spy! After it was proved he was a British airman, he spent the rest of the war as a POW. Future generations should be aware that the world has not learnt much from past atrocities. (Jeanne Hugo)

My mum and her friends at a party with some American servicemen during the war. It captures a moment of boozy freedom and enjoyment – an escape from the oppressive drabness, regimentation and anxiety of day-to-day life in wartime Britain. The girls, all Londoners, had been sent by the government to work at a components factory in High Wycombe, a liberating moment for single girls at that time. Future generations may be interested in the photo as a kind of wartime slice of life, a human and optimistic note amid the general gloom. (Marilyn Francis)

Right: This is a picture of my husband, George, at the age of 16 years in his garden in Sidcup. He was in the Home Guard and was given a rifle and live ammunition to defend our country. This he did until he was conscripted into the 15/19th Hussars, serving in Europe and the Middle East. Fortunately he returned safely and in 1949 we were married. We have just celebrated our golden wedding anniversary. (Mrs B. Oliver)

Above: This is me with my grandmother when we were evacuated from Birmingham in 1941 to Rock, Worcestershire, a significant event which changed the course of my life. I am wearing a green siren suit which was later made into a dressing gown and finally a coat. I have fond memories of riding in a pony and trap, having a pig's bladder for a balloon and suppers of coddled rough cider and a slice of toast to dunk in it. The worst part was having my neck scrubbed when my mother came to visit me. (Anita Bateman)

Right: This photo was taken in 1939 just after the outbreak of the Second World War. My father, Alfred Freeman, is on the left and was in the Territorial Army in the South London Division of the Royal Artillery. Their unit was sent to Oxfordshire. They slept under canvas for many weeks until proper accommodation was available. The photo shows the arrival of the stores. The tins they are holding contain jam – the first thing to arrive for the kitchen. (Betty L. Freeman)

Left: Two WAAF radar operators, off duty at RAF Pevensey in early 1942. The wooden huts were built in the grounds of Herstmonceux Castle (home of the Royal Observatory, now at Greenwich). Because radar masts were a target for enemy attack, RAF personnel were billeted several miles from the operational compound. In 1942, American Army officers came to observe. Then, upon the USA entering the war, 'RDF' (Radio Direction Finding) became 'RADAR'. RAF Pevensey and other radar stations of Fighter Command played a vital part in enabling our fighter pilots to win the Battle of Britain. (Molly Kerridge)

Right: This is a picture of me and my friend at Firing Camp in Anglesey in 1942. We were posted to Portland Bill on Radar, and were there when our troops and Americans went over on D-Day. From our site, we witnessed wave after wave of planes and gliders flying quite low. As we watched them fly overhead, it was hard to describe the feeling – it was partly elation because we felt the end of the war was imminent, and partly sadness knowing that many would not return. My friend and I have kept in touch all these years. (Mrs M. Walker)

Left: This photo was taken in Cardiff during the Second World War. It shows my aunt (seated centre) with members of the local Civil Defence choir. Apparently her husband was 'disgusted' at her showing 'so much leg', which she blamed on wartime skimping of the skirt material. I too joined the Civil Defence in the late 1950s. Years later, it was disbanded, when the nation's fear of air raids finally evaporated. (Brenda Rice)

A double moment of the twentieth century: a young sailor with girlfriend enjoying a spot of leave in Cardiff in 1945 and almost fifty years later, the same couple (my wife and me) enjoying the peace. This peace was fought for by some of the bravest men and women in the world, many of whom died and were unable to reap the benefits of their gallant efforts. But let us never forget their magnificent contribution to the peace obtained in the twentieth century. I regard myself as one of the lucky survivors. (Gwyn Mitchell)

The two children on top of the horse are my brother and me. The photograph was taken during the Second World War while we were staying at a farm in Yorkshire. The farmer's wife opened her home to the families of soldiers stationed at the nearby army camp. The farmer's sons stand on each side of Blossom the farm horse. It shows a bygone way of life, when horses were still used on the farm and also the kindness of people who appreciated the sacrifice fathers were making in being away from home for extended periods. (Irene Williams)

This photo shows the styles worn during the war, at Mum and Dad's wedding in 1939. Grandad (Bill Mawdesley) is at the rear and Uncle Joe and Aunt Margaret at the side. It was usual for servicemen to wed in uniform. My mother Ellen Ann Beckett wore what was available at the time. Silk and such like were in short supply. Dad was born in Darwen and trained soldiers to shoot with .303 rifles in Queens Park, Bolton. Mother was born in Irishtown Ince, Wigan, so-called because of the Irish population employed at the former steelworks. (James R. Beckett)

During the Second World War, my father helped fight the fires of the Blitz. This picture shows the fire crews in their uniforms beside the portable pump. A car was used to tow the water pump which had to be attached to the nearest fire hydrant. It was in regular use when all available fire engines were busy. What a difference to today's equipment! (Mrs A. Heard)

I am not usually the sentimental type, but today (24 July) is the third anniversary of my father's death. Upon learning of *Photos for the Future*, I remembered Dad had thirty pictures from the Second World War, most with hand-written explanations on the back. Having served on aircraft carriers, Dad used to tell me fantastic stories when I was a kid. Maybe kids in future generations will learn the futility of war. *Right*: a 'Hellcat' landing with one wheel. *Below*: Major General Umekichi Urkurda signing the surrender in Hong Kong. (Kenneth Scott)

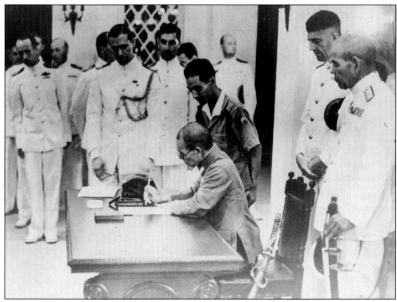

This is a photo of my father (far left), G.E. Beer, the first Admiralty Press Officer in April 1918 conducting a party of US delegates to Clydeside shipbuilders. (Mrs M.J. Wood)

This 1,000 lb bomb was dropped in the back garden of my house – 11 Woodstock Way, Mitcham – on the night of 27/8 July 1941. Luckily, it failed to explode. Nearby were three munitions factories and, just 300 yards from the house, was Pains Fireworks Factory. The photo shows members of 19 Bomb Disposal Squadron, Royal Engineers recovering the bomb. It is believed that this squad was killed shortly after recovering a similar bomb. When it fell, I was looking out of the window at the flares above; the bomb then dropped some 30–40 feet away. I think that must be a record of dicing with death. I was 16 at the time, and as soon as I was old enough, I volunteered for aircrew duties in the RAF. It was much safer. (Vincent Duffy)

On our way back to Egypt after the end of the North African campaign in July 1943, we stopped at Alamein Cemetery. I was able to take four photos. The interesting one is that of the South African officer's grave, on which were fresh floral tributes. I was a TMT Sergeant in 286 Company RASC. We were in Palestine from September 1940 and arrived in the Western Desert on Christmas Day. With only a few months respite, we were in the campaign nearly the whole time, which included some months in Tobruk during the siege in 1941. I am a member of the Rats of Tobruk Association. (Leslie Mizen)

Fifty miles out of Tobruk, Libya, HMS *Grimsby* lists, having been dive-bombed. My great-uncle, Eifion Jones, had been on the bridge and saw three German Stukas 'flying wingtip to wingtip, scream out of the sun'. When the order was given to abandon ship he lowered himself down the exposed side to avoid suction from the sinking. He was rescued from the Mediterranean by the Tobruk pilot vessel *Southern Maid*. He had damaged his leg but recovered in hospital in Alexandria, Egypt. His parents wrongly received a telegram stating that he was 'missing, presumed dead'. (Rhian Jones, Fulford School)

This is Muriel Colyer, during the war. She served in the Land Army and is wearing that uniform. She was a very good friend and neighbour for 30 years but sadly passed away in 1990. A very kindly lady missed by all friends and family. (Mr F. Gregory)

During the Second World War, pin-ups played an enormous part in cheering up the troops. They were known as 'Sweethearts of the Forces' and ranged from film stars to singers and beauty queens. In 1997 the Imperial War Museum thought so much of them that they held an exhibition devoted entirely to 'Sweethearts of the Forces' and photographs of my mother were included. Miss Hammersmith, Miss South London and Miss Finchley were among her titles. She replied to all the letters she received from men in the forces who had seen her picture in the newspapers. Letters came from all over, including active warships and hospitals all over the world. (Caroline Clarkson)

My father-in-law, James O'Hara. He is the driver of the truck. The photo was taken in Tobruk in Libya during the Second World War, where he was serving as a desert rat. I think the photo will be of great interest to future generations to see our British troops at war for our country. (Paula O'Hara)

My mother, Betty Dobbs, 1940, just after the Dunkirk evacuation. She was in the Wrens at the time, posted to her home town of Dover, and is here practising rifle shooting. She has always had a mild and conciliatory nature which makes this scene rather incongruous. But like many other ordinary people then she had strong feelings of patriotism and duty – and might have used this gun if it had been necessary. (Jean Carol Woods)

This picture was taken at Goxhill station, Lincolnshire, in 1945 and shows the last evacuees going home after the war. My mum is on the far right. Two evacuees stayed with her family for several months. Some of the children had never seen green fields, sheep and cows. It seems incredible now that children in this country were taken from their families and sent to stay with strangers. Some children found loving homes, but sadly not all. Today we can't imagine taking children away from their parents. Hopefully it will never be necessary again. (Jo Pacey)

This is a picture of my father who served in the Adriatic in the Second World War. He is the tallest one pictured in the back row. When he joined up as an ordinary seaman in 1939, he entered the lower deck and roughed it in the Atlantic and North Sea, but by 1944, when this photo was taken, he was a Lieutenant Commander. I remember him saying how good Tito was at settling Yugoslavia, but I often wonder what he would say if he knew about the terrible troubles happening again there now. Perhaps in the next century we will have learnt not to let history repeat itself. (Sally Holland)

This photograph of 50 kg German unexploded bombs was taken early in 1940 at Strensall Camp, Yorkshire, where nos 37 and 38 bomb disposal sections were based. Our first job was to locate, excavate and dispose of such bombs at Robin Hood Bay. Fifteen were located, extracted and defused. Their explosive content was removed by taking them to an isolated spot, removing the base plates and inserting rags soaked in petrol, which were lit, and the men retired to a safe place to await either the explosive being completely burnt out or an explosion. Primitive but effective. (Alex E.S. Prentice)

My father, Frank James Gregory, enlisted at the age of 24 on 29 July 1940. The photo showing him and my mother was taken before he left for North Africa on 1 November 1942. Also in the photo is the Regimental diary 1 November 1940 to 8 May 1945 – North African and Italian campaigns, his Soldier's Release book, the medals he earned during the war years and the Rough Riders sweetheart brooch he gave to my mother. This is a little bit of history which I am sure future generations will be interested in. (Mr F. Gregory)

Right: This photo shows some of the horror of war. It is a British 3 in mortar detachment under fire from a German 81 mm mortar and was taken in the desert of Jerusalem during the Second World War. My grandad was a Sergeant with the South Staffordshire regiment: he had a War Office photographer posted with him for some of his time there and the photo was taken by him. (Mr G. Leman)

Left: This is how the *Egyptian Mail* spread the joyous news that the war had finally ended, VJ Day August 1945. (Madge Gegg)

Right: The German cemetery of Fricourt in Northern France. The cemetery contains the bodies of German soldiers who served on the Western Front in the First World War. The picture depicts a German grave and a Jewish grave side by side. Many Jews served in the German Army during the four years of the First World War, but during the holocaust the bodies of nearly all Jewish soldiers were dug up, such was the hatred. However, when the Allies liberated this area of France at the end of the Second World War, they reburied all of the Jewish soldiers in special marked graves such as the one on the left of the photo. I think this photo sums up the millennium because it shows aspects of the two world conflicts: the extreme hatred that could be produced and the forgiveness which allows Jews and Germans to stand together. (Tom Richardson, Fulford School, **Secondary School Winner**)

With the men away fighting in the Second World War, the women had to work to keep the country going. The land girls (or properly the Women's Land Army) worked on the land to grow food for the country. My grandmother was a land girl. She volunteered on 16 September 1940, when she was 17, and left the service on 6 September 1946. The picture shows her in her uniform of trench coat, dungarees, tie and boots, together with her release certificate from the Queen and other memorabilia. (Philippa Mothersill, Sir William Perkins's School)

This photograph shows National Servicemen in the Sinai Desert in 1955 meeting Bedouin children. All males in Britain were eligible for two years' National Service at that time. We were based in the Suez Canal zone. I was a military policeman. I am on the far right and next to me is 'Scouse' Bulman, Irish Guards. I left this magazine with the children and often wonder what it and our visit meant to them. After forty-five years, I still admire their ability to live in such a harsh land. We enjoyed being amateur diplomats for a short time! (Donald F. Morris)

This is one of my happiest childhood memories – the VE Day party at Queen Street, Barry. I was 5 years old (I am the eleventh girl on the right and my mum is the second lady on the left). We had a wonderful day celebrating the end of the war. My dad was on his way home from Africa. I was lucky – some dads didn't come home at all. It reminds me of when families, friends and neighbours looked out for one another. (Mrs P. Poulton)

This photograph was taken in May 1953 and shows the cricket team of HQ Malaya en route to play against a team from one of the rubber plantations in the vicinity of Kuala Lumpur. Here are some of the National Service 'Virgin' soldiers and airmen who played their sport in the best British tradition even if it meant carrying a cricket bat in one hand and a rifle in the other! The sender of the picture is standing third from the left behind the Lance Corporal with the cricket bat. (John L. Evans)

My father, Major C.F.G. White MC. The photo was taken in Malaya in 1956 where the British Army were fighting the Communist insurgents. My father was attached to the Royal Hampshire Regiment. The tiger cub he is holding is one of a pair brought out of the jungle by a patrol. The cubs' mother was unfortunately killed when she attacked the patrol. The cubs were called Rose (after the Tudor rose which is part of the Regimental emblem) and Nasser (which is a regimental battle honour). They were subsequently given to London Zoo. (John White)

This photograph is of me, taken in September 1961 in Leopoldville, capital of what had been known as the Belgian Congo. I was in almost the last intake of National Service and had been posted to Nigeria. Nigerian Independence had passed off smoothly and the new government there decided to send a contingent to the United Nations Force active in the Congo War. It is a marker of the end of Colonialism, both British and European, in Africa, and represents the onset of so much despair in the newly independent African countries. (J.J. Hamblin)

These windows into my family
are three generations of soldiers
who served their country,
through the First and Second
World Wars and finally me in
war-torn Bosnia. Both my
grandfather and my great-
grandfather were injured in the
left arm and although I strive to
be as honourable as them, this is
one consequence I hope to avoid.
I am proud to be a descendant of
these heroic individuals but pray
that one day we can learn from
this tumultuous century in order
that our progeny can live on.
(Michael Ward)

This photo was taken on 21 May 1982 on top of Sussex
mountains in the Falkland Islands – D Day of the conflict. The
story starts in the early hours of 21 May. I celebrated my 21st
birthday in a landing craft. A Royal Navy twenty-one-gun salute, a
bath in the freezing waters of the South Atlantic and a flypast by
the Argentinian Airforce several times bearing unwanted
presents. No party or alcohol but some very expensive and
spectacular firework displays throughout the day. I was a
member of C Company, 2 Para. It was a historic and
unforgettable birthday. Exactly seven days later I was to take part
in the assault of Goose Green – one of the most famous
victories in the history of the British Army. 2 Para were the first
ashore and first into Port Stanley. (David J. Brown)

I took part in the Falklands Task Force
reunion in Gosport in June 1997. It was a
chance to meet up and talk about our
experiences in the war and since. There
were many tales of broken relationships,
unemployment, prison and the suicides of
friends, mentally scarred by what they had
seen there, as I imagine there are when any
group of veterans get together after such a
long time. Not for the first time I
wondered if it had been worth it. The next
day I found this bunch of flowers left by the
children of one of the island's families and
suddenly felt that what we had done not
only meant something in 1982, but was still
important to the people of the Falklands
today. (Tim Lynch)

This is the Berlin Wall in 1990. My husband is taking a piece out of it before it is demolished for ever. We need to explain to future generations what happened in the aftermath of the Second World War, so it cannot be repeated. Russia claimed a part of Berlin and eventually built the wall; the people had to live a life of communism and were not allowed beyond the wall. Anyone who tried to get over the wall was shot and killed, making it literally the Wall of Death. (Mrs M.A. Cooper)

Like a ticking clock, the minutes of this century are marked off in conflicts from local war to global war. My picture depicts the history of these conflicts at the Imperial War Museum. The building was once Bedlam Hospital for the Insane. War too is insane but should not be hidden from view as the Bedlam patients were. We should never forget the wars throughout our history, as we search for peace, so like my picture the guns fall silent. My hope for the new millennium is that with each tick of the clock world peace will gradually become a reality. (Keiron Hammond, Ifield Community College)

This photograph was taken on 6 June 1999 at Dungeness. It shows HMS *Belfast* passing the Point under tow on the way to Portsmouth for refurbishment. If you look at the bow of the ship, you can just make out the towrope. This is the first time the *Belfast* has left London as far as I know since it was berthed there, so there is something here for future historians. (F. Gregory)

Some faces are smiling, pleased to see us here,
But distant there is a barrier, don't get too near,
To the foreign soldier, who is here to stop the war,
Standing in a foreign land, deployed here by IFOR.

I will return home soon, we all go home one day,
But my memories of Bosnia will never go away,
Burnt out houses, bullet shot walls,
And all those different faces,
Is this what the Army meant by 'Visit Exotic Places'!
(David Schofield)

Poppies are regarded as the symbol for remembrance of the victims of war, after they grew on the fields of conflict of the First World War. It's a symbol that should remain into the new millennium to remember those who perished during the two greatest wars in the world's history, those who fought to protect the freedom we have today in this country. Wars should, we all hope, be a thing of the past . . . lest we forget the consequences of such events in history. (Ian R. Judd, **Runner Up**)

A British Army Challenger Main Battle Tank taking part in a night firing exercise on Castlemartin ranges. Less than three months later, it would be firing for real as part of the British contribution to the Allied effort in the Gulf War. (Mr S. Wilkinson)

technology

My father, his granny and their little dog Peter are listening to one of the first sound broadcasts in the world. The year is 1922. My father made the 'cat's whisker' crystal set himself. They lived in Regina Road, Chelmsford. The broadcast came from a nearby village called Writtle, where Marconi had built an experimental transmitter, call sign 2MT. The transmitter was installed in an ex-army wooden hut, now preserved in a Chelmsford museum. Later in the year, transmission was moved to Marconi House, London, with call sign 2LO, prior to the BBC being set up in 1923. (Mrs B.E. Cole, **Winner**)

Diabetes affects the body's ability to control the levels of sugar in the blood. Its discovery dates back to 1500BC when sufferers tried unsuccessfully to live on lettuce and moss. In 1912, insulin injections were discovered as a treatment, but needles were big and painful. This is my diabetic brother, George. He is able to use virtually painless 0.25 mm needles and the latest blood testing equipment which lets him control his blood sugar and monitor his progress on computer. He is hoping that the twenty-first century will bring a cure so he can fulfil his ambition of joining the army. (Edward Hill, **Runner Up**)

Lighting up with Evans Electric. This picture is of great importance to my family. It shows electricity being turned on for the first time in Dinas Mawddwy, Powys, by Rowland Evans, my great-grandfather, using his private generator. The early nineteenth century depended on candles and lanterns. Swan and Edison invented the electric bulb in 1879. Electricity created a great stir when it arrived in the small village of Dinas. The camera captured a moment which changed its history. Dinas moved into the modern time. If it wasn't for the determination of 'Ifans the 'lectric', our lives would be very different today. (Glesni Mai Davies, Ysgol Bro Ddyfi, **Secondary School Winner**)

This picture, itself captured on one of the last technological developments of the twentieth century, the digital camera, marvellously illustrates the continuing life and growth of age-old riverside London. From the ashes of war and following the departure of the once teeming mercantile shipping businesses along these reaches, arise these technological masterpieces. (John Pewsey, **Winner**)

My mum and two of her friends when she was about 14. They are standing by a 'police public call post', which doesn't exist any more. My mum is the one crouching down at the front. These public police phones were quite common at the time this photo was taken, and I wonder why they don't have them any more because they were quite useful. This photo was taken sometime in the early 1960s. The police phone boxes were on most main streets and were used to automatically dial the police in an emergency. (Bonnie Stevens, Maharishi School, **Secondary School Winner**)

The first motorised hearse in Winsford, Cheshire, which my father bought after the First World War. Up until then, he had a horse-drawn hearse and the same horses used to pull the local fire engine until a motorised fire engine arrived in the town. Even then my father was coerced into driving this vehicle on its first call-out as it was only then realised that none of the firemen (all volunteers) could drive. (Betty Rowley, **Runner Up**)

This photo (location unknown) was signed and sent to my grandmother from her friend. It is dated March 1919, just four months after the end of the First World War in November 1918. It pictures Gladys as part of a female munitions workforce, apparently still producing ammunition, presumably to rebuild depleted stocks. Technological advances in the ensuing eighty years have ensured that such a photo would not be possible today as the manufacture of armaments is now mechanised as opposed to 'hand-made'. (Pat Williams, **Runner Up**)

The Sunderland Flying Boat, now history. The photograph was taken from the Hythe Ferry on the Solent. Most were built in Dublin for Coastal Command for the RAF. They also did good service in Norway and Australia ferrying between Sydney and Lord Howe Island. Powered by four Pratt and Witney 1,200 hp engines, all-up weight was 6,000 lb, plus 2,000 gallons of petrol. The aeroplane could cruise at 120 knots for ten hours. It carried bombs, depth charges, gun turrets and beam guns. That was quite an aircraft and the comfort was the best in the RAF. (Gordon Roud, **Runner Up**)

My paternal grandfather and grandmother in London. My grandfather was the Principal of the Home and Colonial Training College for teachers in Wood Green. I'm not sure when the photo was taken, but I would guess at around 1904. What a leisurely time it must have been before the nightmare of modern roads. (Judith Thomas, **Runner Up**)

The aviatrix in the middle is my great-aunt May, the wife of a taxi driver. The photo was taken in about 1918 in a photographer's studio in London. The mock-up of the aeroplane was the nearest that she, or either of her friends, would have got to flying. This picture highlights the extraordinary changes that have taken place this century in the lives of ordinary people. Just after the First World War, hardly anyone would have owned their own camera, let alone flown to Paris. (David Appleton, **Winner**)

A selection of outmoded medical equipment in a photograph from the album of my great-aunt by marriage, Emmeline Beck née Langford. The photo was taken at Highfield Hall, a convalescent home for servicemen near Southampton, in 1917. The theatre has no anaesthetic machine but the dark bottle could possibly contain chloroform. (Dr Jane Richards, **Runner Up**)

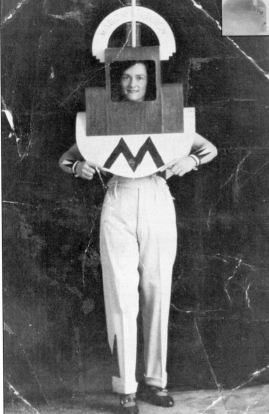

This is my grandmother, entering a fancy-dress competition as a television presenter. The photo was taken in about 1930 when TV was in its earliest days and she seems to have predicted the day when female presenters would take their place in a male dominated medium. She also raised eyebrows because she had to borrow the trousers from a male friend – they were still frowned on as suitable female wear. It was worth it though – she won first prize. (Tracy Eynon)

This is my grandfather, Albert Sanders, in the 1930s, pictured with his home-made radio set. It looks cumbersome and quite complicated. Nowadays, we just press a button to hear sound, and very few of us actually know how it works. I like the idea that, in those days, radio was both an ordinary man's hobby and high technology. (Jane Sanders, **Runner Up**)

One of man's greatest achievements has been powered flight. The pinnacle of this has been the design and construction of Concorde, which has allowed us to travel at over twice the speed of sound in comfort and safety. In 1987, I was lucky enough to win a holiday in Florida on Concorde and this photograph reminds me of the exhilaration of travelling in such a beautiful aircraft. It is unlikely that a conventional plane such as Concorde will ever be built again, because of environmental considerations. (Noel Elkin, **Runner Up**)

Living in Stratford-on-Avon I have seen many visitors taking snaps of the historic Anne Hathaway's Cottage. On 24 June 1999 I witnessed the future technique of taking a still photograph with a film-free camera, held by the owner Jack Reedy, profiled on the left of the frame. A 'snapping' style that will, in the next millennium, commit flash powder, glass plates and bulky cameras to a bygone time. (Willoughby Gullachsen, **Runner Up**)

The closure of the Malton and Driffield Junction Railway in 1958 was a precursor of the massive railway cuts of the 1960s. Not only were the rails removed, but the Burdale Tunnel was then bricked up, an event captured one morning as I was hiking into the archaeological site of Wharram Percy deserted medieval village. Several diggers on this excavation have fond memories of the tunnel; the previous year they had driven through it in a Dormobile to Burdale Station and half a dozen even played tiddlywinks in it by the light of car headlights. (Richard Porter, **Runner Up**)

Our first car, a Messerschmitt KR200, was the result of the petrol shortage caused by the Suez crisis of the 1950s. Amongst many long distance trips was one to Holyhead to get the boat to Ireland. We had to get out every 60 miles to get our circulation back. There was one memorable journey on the M1 from Watford to Luton in thick fog at night, when we were about the only vehicle with a clear view – the fog base was just above the car's height. The final indignity was when someone wrote 'Ban the Bomb' on the roof after a snowstorm. (Roy Bolton, **Runner Up**)

This photograph was taken around the time of the outbreak of the Second World War, whether just before or after we are not sure. It shows a factory involved in the construction of Bristol Blenheim bombers. The factory was Rootes – a car firm – in Speke, Liverpool. The photograph shows how different the manufacture of planes was in those days. My grandfather was working as an inspector and can be seen wearing the white coat on top of the nearest plane in the foreground. Both he and my grandmother are now 93 and living in Horwich, near Bolton. My mother tells me they lived in Liverpool from 1938 but came back to Horwich in about 1940 because of the bombing. They had two children at the time – my mother who was 7 and her brother who was born in September 1939. (Andrew Clarke, **Runner Up**)

The car in the photo is my grandad's Ford Cortina and the person standing next to the car is my Uncle Alan. My granddad didn't have the car long because the whole of my mam's side of the family bumped it, apart from my auntie and grandad, but my auntie wrote it off by reversing it into a lamp post. This photo will be of historical value because it will show how people travelled in the past and the styles of cars used in the 1970s. The building in the background is Teesside University which was built in 1969. (Nicky List, St Clare's School, **Primary School Winner**)

My name is Claire Ferguson and I was born in 1987, eighteen years after man first walked on the moon. This photo opportunity arose when I visited Armagh Planetarium last summer when I was 10 years old. Perhaps I will become an astronaut and send real greetings from space in the twenty-first century. P.S. Neil Armstrong's ancestors came from Broughshane in County Antrim near where I live. (Claire Marie Ferguson)

I chose this photo because it shows some technology at this millennium (a jet engine) and from this, people in the future can see what our engines are like because theirs might be different. (Ryan Peters, Kingfield School)

A Royal Navy submarine. This submarine was in Rosyth Royal Dockyard for a refit and my dad did some work on it. The submarine can hide under the water and would protect us from attack if we were at war. Long ago, there were no submarines and the navy just had ships. This photo would show people in the future how technology has got better over the years. (Andrew David, McLean Primary School)

This is a view of a traditional method used to create the sweetest wine of Jersey – a wine my parents tasted with much enthusiasm! In this century computers and new technology are taking over the world and methods of wine making have now changed so much that Jersey's sweet wine cannot compete with the other wines of the world. This shows that the technology of the early twentieth century did produce good things and although new technology has been adapted to create new wines, will the taste ever be as sweet as the sweet wine of Jersey? (Rebecca Harris, Oak Farm Community School)

My brother relaxing on a railway track! He is not in any danger as it is 18 July 1995 – the day of the National Rail Strike, when no trains ran. The date puts the photo in historical context. For me, its significance is also personally historical. My father and brother were on a youth hostelling holiday after my brother's GCSEs. They walked 60 miles in five days, carrying rucksacks. The photo also makes a comment on public transport – we do depend on it, but when it is not working, we can walk! (Tim Partridge)

Left: This is a photo of my mum in 1973. The car belonged to a neighbour and was parked outside our home in Wavertree, Liverpool. Sports cars are popular today and I am sure will continue to be sought after by future generations. The picture also reflects the fashions of the 1970s. (Julia McAdam)

Right: Tourists in Bristol admire a national monument, the lovingly restored SS *Great Britain*. Designed by Isambard Kingdom Brunel, she was launched in 1843, the largest ship in the world, the first iron ship built as an ocean-going liner. Her honours included crossing to New York and taking the first England cricket team to Australia. Beached in the Falklands by a gale off Cape Horn, she became a coal hulk for five years, then rotted. Rediscovered in 1970, she was brought home to her launching dock of 127 years earlier, a splendid example of early iron shipbuilding. (B. Sheila Redclift)

Left: Oulton Park racing circuit in Cheshire in the early 1960s. The driver is Jack Brabham and his car a Formula 1 car. The comparison with today's Formula 1 racing could not be greater: no advertising on the car, the helmet, the lady on the right with her stop watches and clipboard, the men in their suits, no Grand Prix motor homes, etc. But to me, the greatest difference is the availability of the rider to the public. Try getting this close to Coulthard, Irvine or Schumacher. (Richard Adams)

This is the Millennium Dome, autumn 1998. I have chosen this photograph because I was able to go to Greenwich by boat and look at the dome being built. The Dome is surrounded by many buildings, some of which are of historical value: the Royal Naval College, the Royal Observatory, the National Maritime Museum and Queen's House. The Millennium Dome also stands on the Meridian line dividing the eastern and western hemispheres. The dome may not stand as long as the buildings around it but will mark a significant time in our history. (James Evans, St Simon Stock School)

Above: The disused water wheel of the corn mill in front of my home was just a picturesque photographic object in the 1950s. Then, industrial archaeology was born and it was seen to be necessary to restore and preserve some representative items of our industrial past before they disappeared for ever. The wheel has come full circle, this wheel and the workings of the mill have been restored as a lesson about the past for the future. (Dorothy Rand)

Left: My great aunt took this photo on Avon Dassett Hill, in Warwickshire in 1922. This flourmill was one of two; the first my grandfather remembers being dismantled when he was a boy. His father's explanation for this was that there wasn't enough wind for two! At its apex are my grandfather, Michael Bennett of the Wine Vaults, Banbury, and his friend, 'Uncle' Charles Goldsmith, proprietor of an engineering business in Bow, London. Both mills were in use in the first decade of the twentieth century; this one collapsed just before the war – a beacon stands in its place now. Future technology will never show such beauty and simplicity. (Sarah Holmes)

The giant crane at Finnieston (Glasgow) was fully employed in the early '50s. Large locomotives made in Glasgow would be lined up on the dockside waiting to be lifted and lowered on to one of the many ships tied up at the quay. It was a common sight to see a Clan ship sailing down the Clyde heading for India and all points east. The crane now is no longer busy but one Glasgow car dealer thought it would be a good sales gimmick to suspend one of the latest models from the crane. By the look of it the block and tackle weighs more than the load. (Charles McKirdy)

A small selection of medicines that are in common use towards the end of the twentieth century – tablets, capsules, suppositories all identified by colour and/or numbers supplied by the manufacturers. Towards the end of the century there is renewed interest in more natural remedies – reverting back to the old days? The discovery of antibodies has been one of the biggest helps in combating so many diseases although now we are learning to treat the use of them with caution. All the drugs shown here have been returned for disposal – maybe this is another problem of this century? (Dorothy Burrows)

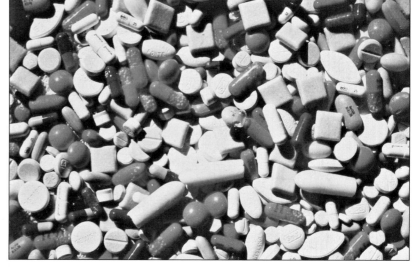

This photo reflects the late 1950s or early '60s. I spent holidays with my grandparents who were very Victorian. When I went to bed in winter, I had a hot water bottle similar to the one in the photo. When I composed the picture in 1995, aged 44, I was studying at evening class for a GCSE in photography – my chosen subject title being 'Myself'. A friend had a collection of stone bottles which she kindly lent me. I arranged them, took and developed the photo and managed to obtain a 'B' grade for my troubles. (Michele Budgen)

This plane, 'The Flying Flea', was designed by a Frenchman and was flown by R. Parker. It was copied by an Englishman, E. Claybourn. Unfortunately, because of a fatal accident, it was grounded and stored. Owing to a hangar fire, it was badly damaged and once more stored. Chief technician, P. Hatton (since deceased), was chosen by a Senior Officer for the honour of restoring the plane. With a team of dedicated workers, it was done and the 'Oakengton Replica Flying Flea' was given the final touches by S.A.C. Duncan. The 'Flying Flea' is now standing in Brooklands Museum. C/T P. Hatton was awarded the BEM. (Mrs E.M. Major)

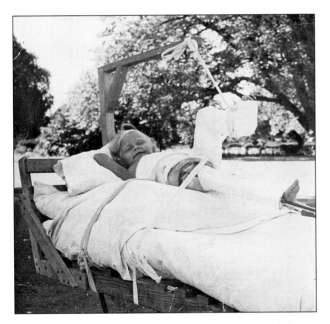

This photograph was taken in the summer of 1951 and shows me aged 4 years in Aston Hall, a country house annexe to Robert Jones Angus Hunt Orthopaedic Hospital, Oswestry. I was born with dislocated hips, and this shows one of the methods of correcting the condition. My mother could only visit once a fortnight. Now, most babies with this condition can be treated at home with a harness to help their hip stay in place. (Susan Sellman)

The last trams operated through the nation's capital in July 1952. With our 5-year-old daughter, we travelled to South London on the last Sunday in July where a No. 36 tram, complete with the words 'Last Tram Week' emblazoned across the sides, was about to leave for the Embankment. It was outside the Trocadero cinema, and as the tram lines are embedded in the road, the conductor is seen switching the points. (Sidney Lipman)

The photograph is of my mother Annie and two friends, Tony and Chris. It was taken in July 1980 when my parents lived on a narrow boat called *Jade*. The photo was taken in Burnley where a number of people gathered to restore a decrepit section of the canal called 'Weavers Triangle'. The main speaker was Brian Redhead who described the north as a 'living museum'. This picture captures a way of life which is growing less common. (Rosie Horsley)

Technology and the advancement of information processing and delivery in the modern world have a large part to play in progress and the evolution of communication. One of the major contributions has been the postal system. During the middle ages, in Britain, only royal households, municipalities, religious orders and universities retained private messengers or couriers. Fees were charged upon delivery and in accordance with distance travelled. In 1837 Rowland Hill proposed prepaid postage (the penny post), laying the foundation of today's postal service. (Ms Christine Davey-Sturman)

In 1953–4 I was a member of the Royal Air Force, stationed at RAF Predannack, Cornwall, near The Lizard. Barnes Wallis and his team from Vickers Armstrong were working on a prototype of a swing-wing aircraft. It was unmanned and controlled by radio. The aircraft was launched from a trolley, on a rail track which was accelerated to about 120 mph and suddenly stopped – this propelled the aircraft into the air. The idea was to steer the craft by moving the wings. The project was not completed as the government withdrew financial support. I believe that the idea was taken to the USA and their swing-wing aircraft was developed from the Barnes Wallis idea. (Alfred Bernstone)

This is the type of fireplace and oven used in my great-grandma's house. Coal was used to heat and cook as there was no gas, electric cooker or central heating. The whole thing would need cleaning and polishing with black lead once a week. Ash needed to be taken out each day. My mother remembers her grandma baking cakes and scones in the oven. She told me food was much tastier from those ovens than our modern ones. It's a shame that they've gone. (Kimberley Daley)

My grandfather in 1910. He stands proudly with his colleagues, dressed in his smart uniform and brass helmet. The horse-drawn fire wagon belonged to confectioners Clark, Nichol and Coombes (Clarnico), but the volunteer officers also dealt with local emergencies. Nowadays we are seeing the emergence of fire brigade vehicles costing £0.5m and being funded by private companies. (Barbara Carlyon)

This photo was taken of me by an unknown RAF pilot in 1943. The aircraft is a Hawker Typhoon which at that time was one of the fastest low level fighter planes used for operational flying. It later became famous after D-Day when it caused considerable damage to the German armed forces. The location was Ludham Airfield in Norfolk; we had just been posted there to help combat the 'hit and run' raids, as well as operations over the North Sea and Holland. I joined the RAFVR in 1941 and obtained my 'wings' in 1942, aged 19. (Mr Kaj Trott)

This is a photograph of my grandad with some of his collection of clocks. He especially liked to hear the ones that chimed on the hour and half hour but it used to take him a long time to wind up the clockwork each Sunday morning before going to church. It was years before I realised that he actually went to the local pub – The Ring O'Bells – which was by the local church. (Joy Edgington)

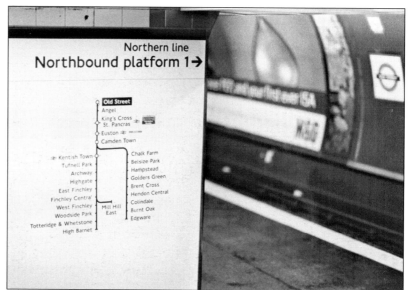

The Northern Line – grotty, run-down, over-crowded, unpunctual but still a technological tour-de-force. It takes a vast army of commuters into town every day and delivers them home at night, and that's no small achievement. (John Carroll)

This is a photograph of a Mini on display at the 1997 British Motor Show at the National Exhibition Centre, Birmingham. The Mini, now owned by German parent company BMW, ceases production in the year 2000. This year, 1999, is the fortieth year of manufacture, longer than any other British motor car. When first on the road in 1959, it was an icon of new technology featuring front wheel drive, transverse engine, a wheel at each corner, interior space and economy. All modern cars have copied, but it is difficult to find anyone who has not owned, driven or been in a Mini and it will long be remembered as a major motoring technological breakthrough in the twentieth century. (Keith Harris)

This photograph shows Concorde, which was a technological breakthrough in the history of passenger aviation. My wife, shown in the photograph, had won this memorable flight as a prize in a competition having said that I, her husband, had always wanted to experience flying on Concorde. Concorde was the first of its kind in both design concept and engineering technology, being capable of attaining supersonic speeds – cutting the journey time from London to New York in half. (Terence Love)

This is my dad leaving Portsmouth on HMS *Triumph* in February 1965 en route to Singapore. You can see the busy naval port in the background and HMS *Victory*'s flagpoles, a symbol of British naval history. Naval ships were bigger and you can see the large crew on the deck; conditions were very cramped and the ship was often at sea for many months. Ships in the 1990s are smaller in comparison, faster and can carry more powerful weapons. Maybe in the future, there will be peace and there will be no need for these ships. (Karen Collinson)

I took this photograph to capture the excitement and sense of anticipation I feel on catching a first glimpse of the Eurostar trains at Waterloo International. The styling of the locomotives, the amazing glazed canopy overhead apparently suspended without support, the cool colours of the station fabric and the gleaming white paintwork of the coaches all project such a powerful image of sophisticated late twentieth-century technology. I can't wait to get on board. (Frederick Hackett)

Left: The government's commitment to helping to provide good quality childcare means that our playgroup must be inspected by OFSTED; this photograph was taken during our most recent inspection in April 1999. Our playgroup introduces children to technology at an early age – the photo shows Sophie, 4, using computer, keyboard and mouse. The member of staff watching is Teresa. (Carolyn Hutton/Janet Kelly)

This is a photograph of the Elizabethan aircraft 'The Lord Burghley' which was involved in the Manchester United Football Club air crash in Munich in February 1957. I took this picture on Sunday 3 February 1957 whilst sitting on the apron at Nutts Corner Airport, which was then Belfast Airport. On Thursday 7 February the aircraft crashed with the loss of many talented football players. This crash is still talked about today, and will always be in the history books of football, both nationally and internationally. I can remember the day of the crash well, and the national sadness it brought. It was the lead story across the media. (Trevor Moffet)

Left: The reason I chose this particular theme was that I feel wind farms will serve an essential purpose in the twenty-first century. We have, over the past ten or twenty years, become more aware of the need to protect our planet, and with this type of expertise, we will be able to ensure the use of environment-friendly energy for many years to come. In the next millennium I hope that more countries improve on this system, enabling governments to sponsor even more energy farms throughout the world in order to put this contemporary natural power saving/producing technology into more homes. (Barry Atkinson)

Winners

Overall Winners

Allen Gaskell, Merseyside; Trevor Williams, Tyne & Wear; Ronald Stuart, West Sussex; Mrs B.E. Cole, Essex; Stu Morrison, West Sussex.

Winners

Karen Braysher, East Sussex; Arthur Colburn, Swansea; Mandy Baker, London; Dame Shirley Oxenbury, London; Robert Vince, Surrey; Sandy Currie, Edinburgh; Anita Varey, Merseyside; James Sammons, West Sussex; John Pewsey, Isle of Wight; David Appleton, London; Eileen Alexander, Essex; Douglas Harris, Hertfordshire; Norman Pitts, Middlesex; Joan Syrett, Middlesex; Jim Kite, London; Matthew Moran, Co. Durham; B.J. Saunders, Kent; Anita Brown, Shropshire; Gwyneth Birkenshaw, Rhondda; Mrs Rita Brown, Yorkshire; Lynda Keld, Hampshire; Brian W. Stephen, East Sussex; Miss Rosie Curran, London; Alan Sams, Manchester; Joan Page, Worcestershire.

Runners Up

Yvonne Marshall, Nottinghamshire; Patricia Skeels, Essex; Sheelagh Davidson, South Yorkshire; Jenny Farmer, Bristol; Gordon Parry, Flintshire; Janet M. Dodson Northamptonshire; Jon Martin, Norfolk; Margaret E. Roberts, Norfolk; Andrew Carreg, Caerphilly; Guinevere Vaughan, Monmouthshire; Mr M.W. Meredith, Gloucestershire; Mr W.H. Watson, Co. Durham; Geoffrey Mayer, Staffordshire; Denis G. Long, East Sussex; Iris Charos, East Sussex; Colin Reid, Berkshire; Franco Scibetta, Staffordshire; Rose Donaldson, Aberdeenshire; Cyril Kellman, Berkshire; Bruce Purvis, Hampshire; Wendy Gowen, Pontypridd; Shirley Sharp, Co. Durham; Marion Pusey, East Sussex; Mrs M. Tompkins, Worcestershire; John Storr, Cumbria; Susan Watson, Belfast; Richard T. Porter, Hampshire; Betty Rowley, Lancashire; Pat Williams, Leicestershire; Mr Gordon Roud, Hampshire; Judith Thomas, Cambridgeshire; Richard Gibson, Perthshire; Dr Jane Richards, Devon; Jane Sanders, Newcastle upon Tyne; Mr N.T. Elkin, Essex; Willoughby Gullachsen, Warwickshire; Roy Bolton, County Clare, Ireland; Andrew Clarke, Lancashire; Mrs J.A. Pike, Cambridgeshire; David Fowler, Middlesex; Mal Martin, Suffolk; Stephen McGinnigle, West Lothian; Alex Stanhope, London; Alan Riley, Lancashire; Mr C.J. Beardwell, Bristol; Jim McCann, Glasgow; David Smith, Staffordshire; Miss I. Bacon, Leicestershire; Christopher Holden, London; Ian R. Judd, Derbyshire; Nicholas Moran, Co. Durham; Jules Thom, Derbyshire; Nancy Vlasto, Surrey; Joan Songhurst, Middlesex; Ruth Sayers, Devon; Beverley Reynolds, West Midlands; June Miles, Essex; John Corrigan, Belfast; Janet A. Stevenson, Gloucestershire; Derek Ross, Dumfries; Ann M.J. Pienkos, Essex; Bob Broadfield, West Midlands; Rebekah Good, London; Dorothy Rand, Co. Durham; Zoë Stead, Lincolnshire; Roger Minshull, Lincolnshire; Mr E.C. Smith, West Midlands; Freda Sheppard, Northamptonshire; Sue Osborne, Leicestershire; Rebecca Smaga, London; Alec Cottrell, London; Tony Boxall, Surrey; Doris Harrison, Lancashire; Roy S. Smith, Essex; Ray Kitching, Co. Durham; Lindsay Heywood, Bedfordshire; Cynthia Dillon, Yorkshire;

Stephen Kornreich-Gelissen, Nottinghamshire; Charles McKirdy, Glasgow; Ray Kennedy, Bristol; Vic Tadd, Cardiff; Euan Bennie, Lanarkshire; Chris Wilson, Dorset; Paula O'Hara, Merseyside; Christine Carswell, Gloucestershire; Gill Mathias, London; Martin P. Lane, Leicestershire; Ann Pope, Merseyside; Gill Barfield, West Midlands; Nicky Lewin, Essex; Oliver Fritz, London; Mr C. Pursey, Somerset; Michael Copsey, Somerset; Barbara Fuller, Wiltshire; Robert Broeder, Middlesex; Mr G.J. Macfarlane, Glasgow; John McWilliam, Co. Durham; Robert Holden, Lancashire; Teresa Quinn, Lancashire; Maureen Epton, Dorset.

The *Express* Winner

Bill Radford, Dorset.

The *Express* Runners Up

Maureen Epton, Dorset; Bob Broadfield, West Midlands.

ntl Winners

Connie Fitzgerald, Hertfordshire; Jean Rundle, Cambridgeshire; Jack Terresfield, Hertfordshire.

Independent Secondary School Winners

Olivia Goodman, Ashford School, Kent; Sam Piper, Brockworth School, Gloucestershire; Charlotte Polland, Castle Rock High School, Leicestershire; Asha Styttard, Coopers' Company & Coborn School, Essex; Kirsty Thomson, Duncanrig Secondary School, South Lanarkshire; Fiona Weir, Duncanrig Secondary School, South Lanarkshire; Lucy Crew, Dunottar School, Surrey; David Dawson, Fulford School, Yorkshire; Bonnie Stevens, Maharishi School, Lancashire; Joe Yoffe, Parrswood High School, Manchester; Katharine Krysula Wright, Pontefract New College, West Yorkshire; Gillian Eunson, Preston Lodge High School, East Lothian; Puja Babbar Queen Elizabeth Grammar School, Hertfordshire; Alex Grady, Reigate Grammar, Surrey; Bérengère Lepine, St Paul's RC School, West Sussex; Daniel Wilcock, St Paul's RC School, West Sussex; Rachel Nicholson, St Wilfrid's CE High School, Lancashire; Richard Mathewman, St Wilfrid's CE High School, Lancashire; Amy Marie Rowlands, The Grange School, West Midlands; Amy Blackwell, The Grange School, West Midlands; Nicola Giles, Tolworth Girls School, Surrey; Sophie F.K. Robertson, Ursuline High School, Essex; Catherine Harrison, Westlands School, Kent; Simon Phipps, Willowfield School, London; Glesni Mai Davies, Ysgol Bro Ddyfi, Powys.

Secondary School Group Winners

Coopers' Company & Coborn School, Essex; Dunottar School, Surrey; Fulford School, York; Kesteven & Grantham Girls' School, Lincolnshire; St Paul's Roman Catholic School, West Sussex.

Primary School Group Winners

St Teresa's RC Primary School, Co. Durham; St Mary's RC Primary School, Kent; St Clare's School, Middlesbrough.